THE *LAZY* KITCHEN GARDENER

by John Yeoman zzz

How to grow MORE FOOD *at home - organically - with* LESS WORK *than you thought possible*

and with MORE FUN!

A Village Guild manual

Published by:
The Village Guild Ltd
The Old School House
Ivinghoe Aston, Leighton Buzzard
Beds LU7 9DP
United Kingdom

Phone/fax: 01525 221492
If phoning from overseas: 44-(0)1525 221492
E-mail: John@villageguild.co.uk

First published 2000
Reprinted 2001

Printed by Antony Rowe Ltd, Eastbourne BN23 6QH.

Printed on chlorine free, environmentally friendly paper from sustainable sources. Guaranteed , in normal use, to perplex VAT officers but not to hurt cuddly creatures or yetis.

ISBN: 0-9542006-0-8

DISCLAIMER

The ideas in this book are given in good faith, and heartily, but neither the author nor publisher nor their agents nor anyone else known or unknown to the author can be held responsible for any use made - or not made - of the information presented here, or not presented. Or of any information that the author *might* have presented or omitted, had he thought to do so. Or even otherwise.

A plea for forgiveness

1.   Please forgive my fascination with **marigolds** and **nasturtiums**, often all too apparent here. Not only do they repel pests, look nice and grow in unlikely soils but they are also, I find, tastier and more nutritious than almost all other salad greens.

2.   I am - it's true - occasionally **repetitious**. Rather than edit out the repetitions, I left them in because - I was pleased to discover - they usually introduce a rather good new idea.

3.   You'll either love or hate the abundant **cartoons** of Mr Yeoman. They're there solely to point a **Tip** or a **Warning**. If you hate 'em, just sprinkle manure water on them and they'll degrade even faster than the author.

> Indeed, *soak* my entire book in water for 24 hours and you can sprout mustard and cress on it. *Steep* it in used cooking oil and it becomes a fierce firelighter. *Shred* and bury it well-soaked under a newly planted potato, runner bean or tomato plant and you'll have a bumper crop...

Sorry. Am I getting carried away, already?

Yours in mulch

JOHN YEOMAN

My printer insisted that this page, for no particular good reason, should be intentionally blank.

Nonsense! To entertain you meanwhile, I thought I would give you a cartoon of myself trying to erect a 7-foot bean trellis, having only a 6.5 foot grasp...

There is a moral in this cartoon.

But you will only fully appreciate its uplifting subtlety, as you go on to read my modest book.

You will, won't you?

WHY THIS BOOK IS FOR YOU

Would you like to grow more food, organically, that's healthier and more nutritious than anything you can buy at the shops?

And to become virtually self-sufficient in essential vegetables, yielding you all the vitamins and minerals your family will ever need? And to do it easily, enjoyably and at little cost - or even no cost at all?

I hope so, because that's the theme of this book.

No garden?

But you may argue, 'I have no allotment, nor even much of a garden'. That doesn't matter, because the ideas here will let you grow more food than you can eat - even without a garden at all!

Is your land hopeless?

If you do have a plot of land that's 'hopelessly' infested with weeds and rubble, don't despair. That was my predicament too, and I'll show you step by step how I solved it - to produce a bountiful harvest.

Do gardening gurus bore you?

If you're tired of glib 'designer' gardeners on television, and coffee-table books and magazines where everything in the garden is always lovely (after a 24 hour makeover), you know the real world is not like that. Perhaps you enjoy experimenting with oddball growing methods, fun and outrageous new ideas you'll rarely find in textbooks but that - perversely - work.

Then this book is for you, a real *gardener*.

Up to a century ago, all the pioneering work of horticulture was done by 'curious' gardeners. He or she (and there were some notable lady gardeners in the 19th century) was usually of independent means, probably an amateur, forever a tinkerer.

It was they who showed how to grow cucumbers, grapes and sweet corn even in Northern English counties and without a hot house.

They discovered that seed saved from different kinds of runner beans, brassica or cucurbits - if they'd been grown together - would not grow true to type. (Though the full explanation would have to wait for modern research.)

They found by trial and error how to bring fresh strawberries, rhubarb, peas, new potatoes and even pineapples to the table in the icy depths of Winter.

I wrote this book for the passionate tinkerer, folk like you and I - the 'curious' gardeners of the *21st* century.

You have, in the best sense, a curly mind.

Your preferred home is the allotment or polytunnel, if you have one. Instead of watching television, you'd rather make a bean trellis out of a child's old play pen or raise heirloom tomatoes in a discarded sink beside the back door. You see nothing eccentric in growing lettuce on the bathroom window sill or broccoli in a wellie boot.

At times, you may have pioneered a breakthrough yourself in gardening techniques.

Don't think for a moment that every major horticultural idea has been discovered by 'experts', still less recorded. I cherish a gardening encyclopaedia from the late 19th century.

Almost everything it recommends as the latest 'scientific advice' - from stripping all the leaves off fruiting tomatoes, and spraying runner beans to help them 'set', to the promiscuous use of soot, lime and salt - is either downright wrong or has long been superceded.

What's more, read a lot of gardening books (as I've done) and you'll find that experts even today continuously contradict each other. Frankly, *nobody* has sufficient experience to lay down the law on what always works best in gardening (or anything else).

Subscribe to serious gardening magazines (you'll rarely find them in newsagents), and you'll see the amazing experiments being explored right now all over the world - in organic hydroponics, companion planting, natural pest control, intensive bed culture, even basement aquaculture.

Most of it is done by amateurs like you and I, just for fun. *And much of it overturns the received wisdom of textbooks.*

May this little book be a catalyst, to help you have more fun and success in your kitchen gardening.

> **PS:** If anyone accuses you of being eccentric, *rejoice!* And refer them to Walt Disney. He was thought eccentric yet he gave us Sleepy the Dwarf, the perfect symbol of the Lazy Gardener.
>
> Surely there can be no greater contribution to human wellbeing in a garden, than the amiable capacity for continual torpor?

WHAT YOU WILL ENJOY...

YEOMAN'S ESSENTIAL RESOURCES

Every lazy or penurious gardener should have these eight essentials readily to hand:

1. A good local pub with a brisk restaurant trade.

This is your primary source of kitchen waste for compost, wood ash from the fire, bottles for Bottle Beds, beer slops for slug traps (well, that's what you can *tell* the publican they're for), and opportunities to barter with the regulars.

In exchange, you can donate the pub all your surplus vegetables except for courgettes, which by tradition are anonymously left on a neighbour's doorstep after dark.

2. A nearby farmer or riding school ...

having ample manure, straw, hay, plastic silage or manure bags to give away.

Barter your organic tomatoes for them, which will be much appreciated. (It is part of the Country Code that farmers never grow their own tomatoes.)

3. A recycling centre, town dump, scrap yard, demolition area or accessible landfill .

Almost everything you need for your garden (even your home) can be found there, from leaves for mulching and old tyres for potato barrels to lumber and corrugated plastic for cold frames. On attended sites, five pounds to the attendant is the going rate for anything worthwhile, I find. Though a large pumpkin once sufficed me.

4. A peacock, to frighten cats off your seedlings.

(Scratch the peacock. Percy, alas, is no more: the victim of road rage.)

5. A farmer's market...

to sell your produce, buy organic seedlings and share gardening ideas with growers who - unlike the pub regulars - actually know the difference between a brassica and a brass band.

6. A garden.

Well, not necessarily if you read this book. A yard, patio, balcony or even an outer wall (or your office car park) will do fine.

7. Indulgent neighbours...

to contribute lawn clippings, leaves, newspapers, beer and cola cans, jam jars and plastic milk cartons, and to receive your surplus courgettes, and to mutter

incredulously over the fence "You won't grow anything *that* way".

8. A tolerant spouse or meaningful other...

who will applaud with convincing sincerity your tomatoes, grown organically in an old laundry basket "they really *do* taste better than supermarket tomatoes, don't they?"

And put up with Grow Poles tangling his/her washing line.

THE SIX RULES OF ROUGH GARDENING
– FOR THE WORST POSSIBLE LAND

How to grow food, regardless, in the worst weed-infested soil

Like to remove weeds from your veggie patch instantly? Just show them a camera.

At least, that's the moral I draw from the deceptive colour photos in the coffee-table books. Nowhere in their lush manicured potagers is seen an ugly weed or a slug-chewn leaf.

It's amazing what a camera can do...

Real gardens aren't like that. Especially mine.

Picture instead a mature 1/2 acre paddock infested with meadow grass, thistles, couch, dock, rape, horse tail... Suppose you want to turn it into a vegetable patch, organically. Would you first rotivate it, so you chop and multiply the roots of those noxious perennials? *No.* (I did.)

Or, following the textbooks, would you mix saladini and radish ("to mark the rows") *in* with your carrot and parsnip seed? So that the former, sprouting vigorously and when pulled, kills the growth of the latter (which was what you really wanted)? *No.* (I did.)

Or mulch your new strawberry plants with grass clippings, and so provide a haven for snails which will *destroy* every single plant? *No.* (I did.)

You'd have been far too wise...

to believe one word of those wretched textbooks. But I was a trusting soul. I'd forgotten that when - 20 years ago - I'd harvested crops galore from a big vegetable

garden year after year, I'd had good, friable weed-free soil to start with. Not a paddock.

Now six months of back pain later (have *you* ever spread 12 tons of manure by hand?) I'm wiser too.

Here are **Yeoman's Six Rules of Rough Gardening (That Work)**. I've personally tested them for the worst case (mine).

Suppose you've inherited a large patch of soil, infested with perennial weeds. Spraying Tumbleweed on it all *seems* like cheating. (Okay, I've done it at times. As *every* organic gardener or permaculturist has, I suspect, when driven to utter despair. Though they'll never, ever tell you that.)

You have neither a martyr's patience to double dig, and burn every weed root you find, nor the time to cover the soil with black plastic and wait 12 months - or five years.

You want crops, *now*.

I assume the soil is in 'good heart'. It has a pH of 6 to 7 and no serious mineral deficiencies, rocks or pollution. (If it's not, there's no option - for quick results, at least - but to overlay it with raised beds and fill them with good imported soil, at fabulous expense.)

Rule 1.   Plant vegetables that laugh at weeds.

This means the big ones - potatoes, onion sets, garlic bulbs, trailing squash and pumpkins, broad beans and jerusalem artichokes.

Beware: the latter, once in, are there *forever*. You'll never dig them all out. Forget about crop rotation in that patch.

Get them into the ground in early Spring and they'll suppress any subsequent weeds or thrive anyway. *True,* you won't get the yields you'd expect from weed-free ground but... would the food calories from that extra yield really replace all the energy you'd expend, weeding to get it?

Weeds also stand little chance against sweet corn, standard tomatoes, chives, miners lettuce, squash, sunflowers (for sproutable seeds), celtuce, land cress, runner and climbing french beans, I find, provided they've been very well started elsewhere. (The same is true of rhubarb, comfrey, fat hen and Good King Henry, if you're lucky enough to inherit them.)

Rule 2. Create your own micro-plots

Sow seeds of chard, broccoli, cabbage, perennial spinach, brussels sprouts and other brassica in traditional rows and, within three weeks, the weeds will have eaten them. *Tried pulling couch grass from a row of seedling chard?* You'll just pull out the seedlings too.

Instead, cut holes in the soil six inches deep and from six to 12 inches apart, according to the width of the mature plant. Set into them collars cut down from plastic milk or cola bottles - six inches deep, open at top and bottom and slit at the side to allow for expansion.

Fill the collars with sterile compost or top soil.

> To sterilise any soil, even horse manure if your spouse permits, put it for 30 minutes in the top oven of an Aga or in a very hot Mark 6 conventional oven, or in a pressure cooker at 15lbs.

Plant two seeds in the collar, an inch or two apart. *Why two seeds?* One might fail but, if both germinate, don't pinch one out (as the textbooks foolishly advise). In early days, you can still successfully transplant one into another collar. And so double your yield.

Plants grow quickly enough this way to resist shading by adjacent weeds, I find, and it's not difficult to pull those weeds anyway without disturbing the collar-protected seedlings.

Important: sprinkle an environmentally-gentle slug and snail deterrent into the collar immediately after planting. Or the snails will crop that seedling before you even see it.

Sharp sand, grit or wood ash are often advocated in textbooks as snail-deterrents, but after a heavy rain they don't work. Instead, paint a thick band of used cooking fat or vaseline, mixed with salt, on both sides of the collar rims - and renew it regularly. It works.

A friend vouches for collars cut down from 'own label' cola cans. Their razor-sharp edges repel slugs and snails, he claims. I suppose they'd still be friendly to the environment, if not to your fingers - if you remembered to remove them later.

A Tip: string them together then, at the end of the season, you can pull them all out - together.

A mollusc repellent that also did wonders for me were the abrasive surfaces of plastic scouring pads. You can buy job lots of these pads for mere pence from market stall suppliers and they'll last you till the next millennium.

Forgive me, if I go on to repeat these mollusc-repelling ideas. *Slugs and snails kill gardeners.* At least, they kill their morale. So I make no apology for returning to this topic in greater depth, elsewhere.

Another micro-plot that works is a long gutter.

Hoe a trench six inches wide and deep. Put in a gutter made from folded thin card or thick newspaper. Fill with sterile compost or soil. And scatter your seeds. The card or paper will have rotted away by the time the roots need depth. Meanwhile, the weeds can't get in.

A tip when all fails: you can grow potatoes *anywhere* in large manure or rubble bags, perforated and filled with a mixture of rotted manure and rough soil. Set the chitted potatoes on a foot or so of this, cover them with a few more inches, then keep adding soil - or even straw - as they grow.

> I tucked eight bags in March behind the paddock fence, where they disappeared into the weeds. I took out the new potatoes in June and replanted those bags - now full of rich, 'cleaned' humus - with peppers and cucumbers.

Rule 3.   Mulch between transplants with card or newspaper

It's a fool's paradise if you think you can clear a plot temporarily and drop in the more delicate transplants, like brassica. The weeds will creep over them in days.

Swiss chard growing well in a card gutter, despite weeds

Instead, lay card or thick newspaper between the transplants.

When I tried this one February, high winds blew my cardboard into three counties. So in May I laid kitchen waste on it to keep it down and it worked. ('Mulching' with wooden planks worked too, in the absence of an old carpet.)

However, snails lurking under the waste and planks devastated my first transplants. The remainder survived, only after I protected each with a little mat of rough sandpaper ringed with grease.

> **Moral:** don't mulch transplants unless you apply an effective slug and snail deterrent, the very moment you plant them. (Yes, I repeat myself - but it's *important!*)

Rule 4. *Don't sow dainty small seeds like carrots and parsnips in traditional rows*

They won't grow fast enough to resist invaders nor, in weed-infested soil, can you weed them effectively. Those determined to grow carrots, parsnips, beetroot, celeriac, skirret and other roots in weedy soil could start them individually in compost-filled loo rolls.

Plant the entire roll. When the plants are well-established - the card rots away.

> **A tip:** it takes several weeks for loo rolls to rot, so reserve their use for crops that will be in the ground for some while.

Or you could use Rootrainers, transplanting the mature plugs (see later).

A lazy-gardening tip that worked with my carrots is: don't plant them in rows at all. Just scatter the seed of a short-stumped variety thickly over a cleared bed. The resulting dense foliage, I found, suppressed even dock and couch.

I fed the early thinnings to the guinea pigs - filling in the holes to avoid luring carrot fly - and was left with a bumper crop of good-sized carrots.

 A Tip: Fast-growing short-stumped carrots make a great weed suppressant *anywhere* in the garden. The fronds look pretty too. Perhaps this might work with other tubers?

Rule 5.   Eat your pests

When wild turnip (rape) invaded my paddock, I culled the younger leaves and cooked them - with young nettles - for 10 minutes in a little stock, plus fresh marjoram and lightly fried onions, and had a delicious side dish. Indeed, I cooked an ovenful for the freezer too.

Dock and couch aside, could you *eat* your pests?

English gourmets once swore by garden snails, wall apples, 'cleaned' for three days by feeding them on flour then baked in garlic butter...

Rule 6.   So your garden still looks like a jungle?

Relax. I became almost clinically depressed in the early months of weed invasion till I realised - I'm never going to have a garden like a coffee-table book anyway. But as I don't write such books, who cares? Meanwhile, I'm eating heartily out of my jungle, using the ideas above.

That said, this Autumn it's total war.

I'm going to swathe my entire paddock in black plastic. Next spring, I'll cut little holes through the plastic, drop in transplants grown in my conservatory (including carrots and parsnips), and blanket that plastic in sand paper, grease bands and scouring pads.

(Is that what folk mean by a *'kitchen'* garden?)

Weeds, slugs and snails... eat your heart out.

 Footnote: Since I first wrote that, I actually went on to do it. But with interesting variations. I'll tell you about them, as you read on...

BOTTLEBEDS - A NEW YEOMAN BREAKTHROUGH?

How a free Bottle Bed grows you earlier plants, decoratively... and warms you too!

Ever wanted to grow tomatoes, squash, beans, sweetcorn or indeed almost anything - so it matures as much as a month earlier than normal?

In our grandparents' time, the secret was to grow them over a hotbed. A deep pit of raw manure and straw was dug below a cold frame so that, as it rotted, it heated the plants grown above it. So in late Winter or early Spring, the cold frame became a hotbed. Forced strawberries, rhubarb and other delicacies could be brought to the table at unseasonable times.

Once its purpose was served in forcing early plants, it cooled and became a conventional cold frame again to harden off transplants. In Summer, that rich compost in the cold frame would also grow any muck-loving plant, like courgettes, marrows, pumpkins, tomatoes or beans. By Autumn, it could be forked out to enrich the rest of the garden.

Yet most of us don't have a riding stable next door to our gardens offering unlimited free manure and rotted straw.

Plus a peacock who flutters in daily, to deliver his own super-rich droppings, and scare cats off our seed beds...

Well, actually, I'm lucky enough to have both and the peacock's name was Percy. Till he collided with a milk truck. *But I digress...*

Solution? A Bottle Bed!

This idea is fun because, to fully understand its awesome potential, you should first drink 12 bottles of wine. At that point, everything will seem awesome and you will view your garden from an entirely new dimension. So don't attempt this strategy until the next day...

You now have a clear head. Right?

You also have 12 empty bottles - ideally dark-glassed - with corks. Fill them with water and replace the corks. Next, locate a robust wooden tray, floor tile or board about 1 ft square, or a large clay or plastic saucer of around 15in diameter. This is the base for your Bottle Bed.

Tie 10 or 12 bottles together in one long bandolier using a strip of industrial packing tape. (Ordinary sellotape disintegrates in weeks.) Tape it front and back so those bottles are firmly strapped into one long line. *Or* tie them together with wire or string.

Of course, anybody who watches BBC's Ground Force will weave those bottles together with white marine rope at £5 a yard, having first painted the bottles blue...

Arrange the bottles on the base in a circle and secure the first and last bottle so you now have a round-sided container.

Finally, put an inch or so of polybeads, broken polystyrene board or gravel (tightly-balled newspaper is better than nothing) at the bottom for drainage. This is essential if you use a saucer, in which water will gather. And fill the Bottle Bed with compost.

> **A tip:** in a drought, a saucer will save you having to water quite so often.

How to fill a container

Everyone has their own ideas about how a container should be filled, so I won't be dogmatic.

A lot depends on what you intend to grow. For tomatoes and other heavy feeders, I like putting two inches of rich home-made compost at the bottom, then two inches of sifted garden soil mixed liberally with wood ash, and the final inches topped with shop-bought compost to deter weeds.

It's cheaper than using purchased compost for the lot and, by the time any weeds emerge from the unsterilised soil, the tomatoes (etc) will have grown vigorously enough to suppress them.

Alternatively, use a mix of compost and topsoil and suppress those dratted annual weeds by covering the container top lavishly with strips of cardboard. Then sprinkle purchased compost over it to disguise it.

You could add a handful of water-retentive granules, though that's costly and not justified if you water daily.

> I found they swelled so much they pushed my plants out of the pot. But being fuddled by 12 bottles, I doubtless added too much...

Some folk bury banana or other fruit peel, or old tea bags or coffee grounds at the bottom of their containers. All help retain water while the fruits add potash.

> *Or* mix in a small handful of wood ash - if you haven't done so already - for potassium-loving tomatoes and cucurbits (that's cucumbers, courgettes and squash, for us peasants). Wood ash or soot sprinkled around the root ball is also said to deter boring insects from any plant.

Enough of this alchemy...

Now wrap the bottles with anything that will stop the wind and rain from drying or leaching out the compost. A strip of old carpet, bamboo blind, hessian sacking or table matting might please those of a delicate sensibility.

(Scour your local recycling centre or charity shop.) The rest of us will opt for plastic strips from manure sacks.

Carry your Bottle Bed to its intended location in the garden.

> *Whoops!* I forgot to tell you. It's very heavy. So best fill those bottles with water, only *after* you've moved them to their permanent location.

Plant in it your hardened-off early tomato transplants, or any other large plant to which you want to give a month's jump start. Stick a bamboo cane in one of the bottles as a support, if necessary. Or stick into the bottles three or four slim willow, elder or hazel poles - even some more bamboo canes - and tie them at the top.

"We're not in *that* much of a hurry to make a bottle bed!"

Now you have a Bottle Bed Tipi!

It's ideal for growing beans, Sweet Williams, nasturtiums, cucumbers or other climbers.

Then keep the container moist, ideally with ambient-temperatured water from a garden butt.

> **A Tip**: if you erect a tipi, *tie* the bottles to the base with cord. Or wind may topple that precarious edifice. I speak from experience...

Why go to all this trouble?

Well, your Bottle Bed is free - whereas you might have paid up to £50 for a similar-sized decorative container at the garden centre. And you must admit it's pretty, especially if wrapped in table matting recycled from a council skip. It's a conversation piece for your friends, not least if you invite them to join you in starting another Bottle Bed.

 Wine is cheaper by the case, of course, so buy lots of cases. *For your Bottle Beds...*

And frankly, to make one Bottle Bed from scratch will take you all of 15 minutes. (I made 20, enough to fill my patio, in less than a day.)

Why does a Bottle Bed grow plants quickly?

Seriously... those water-filled bottles act like **heat traps**. They absorb solar energy during the day and radiate it back at night - into the roots of your growing plants.

Designers of energy-efficient homes have built entire walls out of empty wine bottles, even beer cans, precisely for that purpose. It takes just a few degrees of extra soil warmth to give plants a big spurt.

You also have some protection against the worst effects of a late frost, especially if you shroud the foliage as well with fleece, bubble wrap or a plastic kitchen rubbish bag on frosty nights.

In my own unscientific tests, in the 1970s (when I still thought the Beatles were a garden pest) the Bottle Bed yielded me red tomatoes as early as mid-June - when my neighbours were still watching the first trusses forming.

Once you have the Bottle Bed habit, you'll find lots of other garden uses for those bandoliers of empties. **Sink** them half-way, upside down, around your lawn or veggie beds as edging. **Bury** them to their base, upside down, in pathways. (It's very decorative if you use different coloured bottles; at least, until they get smashed...)

Make **big** Bottle Beds four or five foot square to grow courgettes, pumpkins and other sprawling plants that use up a lot of precious space in the ground. I have successfully raised a wheelbarrow-full of fat carrots and parsnips in a big Bottle Bed, each grown together far, far tighter than the textbooks allow.

And yes, I'd *transplanted* those carrots, by first growing them in loo rolls!

> **Note:** a 1ft high raised Bottle Bed is also virtually immune from low-flying pests like carrot flies, and far less likely to be bothered by molluscs.

Carrots growing in a big Bottle Bed - and yes, they were *transplanted* - using loo rolls

You can build a Bottle Bed even on a concrete forecourt!

What's more, you can make a Herb Spiral. Mount the bottles in a spiral, with each at the perimeter buried one inch less deep than its neighbour and the final bottles at the centre raised above ground on bricks.

Then fill your circling bed with compost to form that sacred emblem of shamanic gardeners (and permaculturalists) - a Herb Spiral. And very beautiful it is.

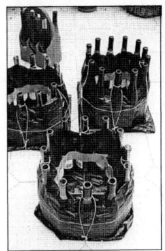

> Even if you're not concerned about getting early vegetables, Bottle Beds make novel, attractive - and free - growing containers for *flowers*.

In the unlikely event you *don't* want to drink 12 bottles of wine, you'll get empties galore from pubs and restaurants - if you promise to return them a few fresh early tomatoes, organically grown.

Lusting after organic tomatoes, my local publican now drops 12 empties a day on my doorstep. *How many bottle beds can a man make*, I ask? And mine's just a tiny village hostelry. If you live in a city, your bottle supplies should be inexhaustible...

I'm sure water-filled beer cans would prove effective heat traps as well, but in the interests of your sensibility I won't pursue here the topic of a *Budweiser potager*...

HOW TO GROW A SIX FOOT BEAN PLANT N A 15 OZ BAKED BEAN CAN

Okay, I lied.

Let me now introduce you to the ultimate low in Bottle Beds - a *Budweiser potager*.

Except that, I don't drink Budweiser. I prefer to rinse my hair with it, to dispel dandruff. It has no other use, has it? (And don't jest: beer shampoos actually *work*.)

So instead, I used cola cans. I built little **Cola Beds**, inserted a 15oz baked bean can in the middle (a 440 ml or 3/4 pint beer can would have done as well), and grew runner beans in it - taller than myself. All on my patio.

Yes, you *can* truly grow almost any climbing plant in a baked bean can and harvest many pounds of produce therefrom. On your porch or balcony, without a garden at all.

You simply borrow a trick from Ring Culture.

Ring culture? Let me digress from Cola Beds for just a moment...

As you know, tomatoes are often grown in greenhouses to improbable heights in a container 9 inches wide and 10 inches deep made by stapling a sheet of lino, carpet, roof felt (even our old friend, manure bag plastic) into a ring, open at both ends.

> **Tip:** an even easier idea is to take a big plastic flower pot, cut out its base, and turn it upside down.

> It can even be put on top of another, more shallow flower pot, so doubling its depth.

> A double pot is *wonderful* if you want to grow beans in minimal space, or over-leggy tomatoes. It's very efficient because, when you water the top pot, you can't help watering the bottom pot too - where the roots are.

Forgive me if I touch on this later but a good idea is worth repeating. (Or have I said that before?)

This pot is filled with compost or sterilised topsoil and set upon a ditch or tray filled with gravel, cinders, sand or other loose sterile aggregate.

Wood bark, cocoa shells, sterilised soil, sawdust or wood chips work nearly as well as a base, and I've used them all. You can re-use them on the garden as mulch next year.

The seedling is set deep in the pot when some 8 inches tall and, after the compost has been watered for a few days to help the roots grow, all water thereafter is directed into the aggregate.

The roots grow sideways into the compost, then down and out in search of water. And, because the aggregate is kept continuously moist with water and nutrient feed, the plant grows even better than it might have done in soil.

This is a hybrid form of hydroponics.

Some say it's a *superior* form because the compost will supply the plant with additional trace minerals (some of which we may still be unaware of), that are not present in a manufactured chemical solution.

Meanwhile, the nutrient food ensures the plant gets an ample basic diet, including moisture, so it needs far less root growth and can put its energies into fruit or leaf formation.

That's **Ring Culture**.

Of course, Yeoman's strategy goes way beyond (or, rather, below) Ring Culture. As you'd expect...

Let's call it... Ring-Pull *Culture.*

You simply use **cola cans**. You can build little Cola Beds just one foot in diameter or (I've no doubt) Beer Beds the size of a soccer pitch, if you wished. (Scour the pitch after a match and you'll find enough beer cans.)

The perimeter consists of empty cans.

Their tops are cut off and a panel around two inches deep by three inches wide is cut open half way down the side. A quality can opener makes a neat job of the tops while kitchen scissors will slice open the thin sides of most cola or beer cans.

 Beware: wear gloves. Those ragged edges are razor sharp!

Band the cans into a ring with industrial adhesive tape or string and place on a sturdy board. Fill the centre of the ring with gravel or a similar aggregate to a level that just covers the open panels in the cans.

If your gravel tends to be more than a half-inch wide, mix in an equal quantity of builders sand or vermiculite to retain the moisture.

Make sure the bottom of each perimeter can is also filled with a similar aggregate so it's weighted down and makes a sturdy frame. Put one or more further cans, each cut open at the tops and sides in a similar way, in the centre of the Cola Bed. These are the cans you grow plants in.

You don't need vast depth

Good results for most climbing plants can be had using 15 oz or 440 ml cans.

If you sink several of them in a row four inches apart you can successfully grow runner or climbing french beans in a long narrow trough just eight inches wide and in as little as three inches of gravel. If they're planted outside, just be sure to secure the base firmly eg. with breeze blocks. Or

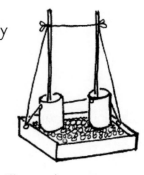

one puff of wind, and that tall trellis will topple over.

> Hydroponicists typically grow vast plants in even smaller containers - but then, they're using technology equivalent to a hospital life support system.

You don't need high-technology

For amateurs like us, the larger and deeper the can, the better, because the deeper is the tray, the less frequently it must be kept watered.

But tomatoes and beans have short roots. Given enough moisture and support (and provided their roots are kept dark), tomatoes, beans - and many other plants - can thrive with virtually no root depth at all... just using a capillary mat.

Fill the central cans with gravel up to the top of the cut out panels in the can sides. And insert a transplant on top of the gravel. The rootball of a tomato or bean plant grown in a standard three inch pot can be gently squeezed into the cut open top of a beer can without damage.

For smaller transplants, fill the top half of the can with compost and insert them (holding the lower leaves *not* the stem) in the same way as you would pot on any seedling.

Water the compost for a few days to spur new root growth, then every day direct the water instead to the aggregate. Fill the Cola Bed to the brim with water.

If you've set the cans on a board, the water will drain away quickly by itself. That's fine - the roots need air as well as moisture and would drown in an undrained bed.

If you've put the cans around the sides of a drawer or other solid container, *you've been thoroughly lazy* (and I applaud you for it). But now you'll have to empty out the gravel to drill drainage holes in the base of the container. And you'll have to start all over again, *won't you?*

 Moral: do read my modest instructions here, first...

Every day (and more frequently in very dry weather) water the tray. And every two days or so fill the aggregate to the brim with a nutrient solution. Remember, the plants won't be getting much nutrient from the little amount of compost in their cans.

The regular application of liquid fertiliser is not just a wise option (as in soil-based culture) but an absolute necessity with ring - or **ring-*pull*** - culture.

What feed do I use?

Use a proprietary **potassium**-rich liquid feed - like Phostrogen Tomato Feed - for tomatoes, beans, cucurbits and almost any fruiting plant. But use that potent feed only *after* the plants have set their first trusses or flowers.

Some textbook authors advise you feed a potash solution *before* the tomatoes set fruit, but not after. Some advise exactly the opposite. It just proves... your own gardening experience is worth a library of those wretched authors.

What I *do* know, from experience is:

> A rich feed solution, added too early, produces lavish leaves but little fruit or flower. That's fine if you want to grow eg. nasturtiums or marigolds for their deliciously edible leaves alone. The leaves grow as big as dinner plates. One giant nasturtium leaf with mayonnaise makes a sandwich. *But it's no good if you want flowers or fruits.*

Follow the manufacturer's dilution instructions for root or ring culture feeding. If you want to be totally organic, fertilise instead with a balanced **comfrey-nettle** or **manure tea qv.**

Hydroponic purists will have an entire laboratory-full of exotic nutrient solutions, varied for every type of plant and also for different phases in its growth. But **Ring-_Pull_ Culture** is merely a modest, _hybrid_ form of hydroponics and the above will serve us well enough.

The extended Cola Bed

Of course, there's no need to neglect those empty cans round the sides. To make full use of the Cola Bed, fill them with compost and insert small edging plants - lettuce, marigolds, nasturtiums, parsley, strawberries, aromatic herbs...

Even dandelions. Disdain them not. They're about the fastest edible plant you can grow. A small piece of root in every can will give you almost instant decorative edging.

> Eat the young leaves in salads, _or_ put a plant pot over them for two weeks to blanch the older leaves so they're succulent and free of bitterness (_delicious!_ that is, if they don't rot instead or the slugs don't get 'em). _Or_ steam or stir fry the flower heads.

> **A tip:** grow dandelions quickly indoors from pieces of root then snip the young leaves into salads.

> Just don't let them go to seed or they'll colonise the entire garden... or your house.

If you fill the corner cans entirely with gravel, you can set small canes in them, tethered to the base with string, to serve as supporting tipis for climbing plants.

At the end of the season, sterilise the aggregate in a hot oven for 30 minutes or rinse well with a weak solution of bleach and bag it up for use next year. (Or use for **indoor hydroponics** *qv,* which I touch on briefly elsewhere here.)

Bonus: make a free bird-scarer too

Don't waste those shiny pieces of metal you cut out of the can sides and tops. String them above your veggies as effective bird scarers.

Do likewise with those dratted free CDs that Internet firms insist on mailing you. They make wondrous wind-chimes for a child's playroom and, with lights shining on them, also bring you - en famille - your very own *Son et Lumiere!* But perhaps I digress...

A plastic milk jug Grow-Pot

The Cola Bed is akin to the growing containers used by office landscapers to grow decorative indoor plants. The plants root in a mix of compost and expanded clay pellets, fed constantly by a water reservoir.

You can easily improvise these Grow-Pots with plastic milk bottles.

For one pot, you need three 4 pint plastic bottles. Cut one in half, about an inch above the bottom of the handle. Cut another one into an open-ended sleeve of the same depth. Insert the open-ended sleeve between the top and bottom of the first container.

Tape them together using heavy-duty waterproof adhesive tape so you have one deep pot about 12 inches tall.

Perforate the base of the tall pot for drainage and cut two panels each around two inches wide by three inches deep in one side.

This is your growing pot.

Take the other shorter pot and drill a line of quarter inch holes down one side, with several holes bunched toward the bottom.

This is your watering pot.

Position them so the drilled holes on the watering pot face into the cut open panels on the growing pot, glue the two cut sides together with waterproof adhesive and wrap industrial tape around the two pots from top to bottom to secure them as one unit.

Put a half-inch of small gravel at the base of the growing pot then fill it with a mix of compost and vermiculite (or other filler to assist drainage) and ensure the compost presses tightly against the watering holes. Insert the plant.

Place the container on a drip tray, if it's to be housed indoors. Fill the watering pot.

According to the size and number of the holes, the watering pot will drain into the growing pot in a minute or two - thoroughly saturating the compost from top to bottom.

> If you're growing tomatoes or other tall plants, use the convenient hole that's left from the jug handle to insert a cane.

To stop the unit toppling over, tether it to a wall. To make it look attractive (and also shade the roots), wrap the unit in - *yes, why not?* - that awesomely versatile thing, black manure-bag plastic.

Provided the watering pot is filled daily, and nutrient feed used twice a week, the compost will stay moist enough to grow a substantial plant.

> To my astonishment, when I did this, my tomato plants grew around twice as many tomatoes as similar transplants I'd set in clay pots at the same time - but using about twice as much compost.
>
> I can only conclude, it was because the reservoir-watered pot got more water.

A variation on this is a Grow Tray.

Simply take nine plastic milk jugs. Cut them to half size.

Thread them together with plasticated string into a tray, six half-jugs on each side and with one jug in the middle to serve as the water reservoir. *(See diagram.)*

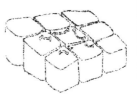

Cut a drainage hole in the corner of each outer pot, toward the tray center. (But, this time, *don't* fill the bottom of each pot with gravel or poly beads for drainage. The reason will shortly become clear.)

Lay a piece of capillary mat on the base of each outer pot. The mat has a long slim tendril which snakes up and drapes into the central pot. The central pot is the **watering pot.**

Fill each outer pot with a mix of compost and sand or vermiculite. Water it well. Be sure the whole capillary mat is soaked.

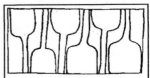

How to cut capillary mat. Lay the large ends at base of the grow pots and drape the thin tendrils over the sides and into the central reservoir.

Plant your seeds, such as lettuce, herbs or even alpine strawberries, in the outer pots, watering them just enough to keep them moist. (If you do this indoors, better put a tray underneath.)

Transplants can be dropped right in, if the roots touch the mat. Shroud the sides of the pots in black plastic, or else sunlight will turn the interior soil a delicate algae green.

As soon as they're growing well, stop watering from the top - and just keep the central water reservoir topped up.

This simple idea can yield you an abundance of lettuce and other plants year-round, indoors. You can make and plant a Grow Tray in 15 minutes. It then takes 3 seconds to top up the reservoirs, once every three or four days.

Why bother to build a Grow-Pot or Grow Tray?

Couldn't we just stick our plant into the grow-pot or tray and top-water it?

No! Had you simply inserted your transplant into that tall Grow Pot, without using an adjacent watering pot, and watered the plant from the top you'd have had... merely *micro* plants. Or no plants at all. The water would not have reached their roots.

This way, you can grow plants almost as big as you wish, anywhere, indoors or out. In a negligible ground area.

And had you just planted seeds in individual half milk jugs which dry out in a day, instead of a Grow Tray, you'd be *forever* watering them. Instead, of doing it just twice a week.

Now you can take a very long weekend's holiday, without feeling wretched meanwhile (I know you would) about your thirsty seedlings...

Is this yet another triumph for plastic milk bottles?

Nine ingenious 'breakthrough' cloche ideas to raise any plant, almost anywhere

My favourite cloche is big enough to hide me, *plus* a case of wine which I'm emptying solely to furnish my Bottle Beds (of course) *plus* the Sunday newspaper.

Every mature gardener knows the value of giving young plants (and themselves) protection against pests. These may include insects, cats, children, unexpected visitors or spouses.

Indeed, some allotments seem to be a makeshift tent city of protective bird, rabbit or cat netting, carrot fly screens and polytunnels (wherein cups of tea or the odd Guinness can be discreetly supped).

A cold greenhouse is the ultimate plant protection short of a hot house or conservatory, but it's expensive. And fiddling constantly with screens, ventilation, shade paint and watering cans to avoid plants frying, freezing or wilting is for me - the world's laziest gardener - **hard work**.

Instead, here are ideas for home-made cloches that repel birds, molluscs, pets, small children, ducks, spouses, monsoons, gales and yetis*... but cost little or nothing, either in cash or labour. They retain humidity or admit enough rain so - short of a drought - your watering chores are minimal.

1. Corrugated polytunnels

Re-cycling yards sometimes abound with corrugated clear plastic which can be curved into a tunnel, tethered to the ground with stakes and string and blocked at each end with boards - or ideally sheets of flat perspex.

> Working with sheet glass in the garden is just too hazardous, I think, unless it's sturdily framed.

Trouble is, unless you've inserted a leaky pipe, the sheet must be continuously removed for watering.

Clear thin polythene can also be stretched over a wooden frame, its sides buried to repel molluscs and its top surface perforated to admit rain. But this weakens it and a gale will shred it. There are better ideas below...

2. Pyramid cloches

Clear rigid plastic is absurdly costly in the shops but offcuts can be had **free** for the asking from many plastic suppliers or fabricators. Merely a broken corner or scratch may make a sheet unsaleable but it's fine for our purposes.

Cut those sheets into three or four equal sized triangles.

It's easiest to use a Stanley knife with a no. 5194 blade but an electric saw with a fine toothed blade works, if the sheet is clamped firmly between two wooden boards.

Drill a half dozen 1/8in holes in the middle of each triangle, spaced well apart. (I find a cordless drill, set to low speed and using only light pressure, avoids cracking.)

Then drill a line of holes, about 2 inches apart, a half-inch in from two edges, leaving one edge undrilled. (The edges are fragile so this is best done by clamping thin lathes on either side and drilling through the 'sandwich'.)

Lace each vertical edge of the pyramid together using string or raffia, so that it hinges into a pyramid. Secure the last edge with only a twist of wire or two so this sheet becomes an openable 'door'.

Now you have an elegant cloche that would grace a window sill.

It can be made quickly in any size, according to what offcuts you have available. Molluscs and other pests can't readily get in, if you bury each side an inch in the soil.

This is also important to retain heat and moisture; otherwise, gaps will create an undesirable funnel effect and blast out the warm air.

Rain and air can penetrate the perforations but the structure is massively robust - even a gale is unlikely to topple it. Plants can easily be set out or harvested by opening the door. It will also fold flat for storage.

3. Cone cloches

If you're lucky enough to find a low-cost source of very flexible clear fibreglass, cut it into a semi-circle, with a

semi-circular gap at the top three inches in diameter. This becomes a hole for ventilation. Then roll the sheet into a cone. Overlap the sides by an inch and secure them with rivets or tight wire loops.

> I have not tested this, but a US grower claims the cones help him raise crops all Winter despite snow and storms, last almost forever and can be stacked for storage.

When you spot these clever simple cloches being sold in garden centres - at £50 each - remember you first read the idea here.

4. Bamboo cloches

You can make a simpler variation in moments. Obtain four builders rubble sacks, the kind made with translucent ultra-tough plastic. (Alas, it may have the manufacturer's name on one side; hence the need for four sacks to get four clear sides.)

Cut each into a triangle, leaving space for a two inch gusset on each side and a ventilation/watering hole at the pyramid's top.

Lay bamboo canes at each edge, using eight in all, and fold the plastic over them, sealing the seams with all-weather tape. Drill a small hole in the ends of each cane.

Then it's simple to construct a pyramid: tie together the canes where they all meet at the apex and thread together each pair of canes at the bottom.

> This gives less protection against mollusc invasion, unless you seal every gap with weatherproof tape. It also must be tied down with stakes at each corner, or it will turn into a kite at the slightest breeze and vanish into the next county.

> But it protects young plants from the elements, and cats. You could even double-insulate the pyramid, for greater frost protection, by using *two* sheets of plastic per side.

Simpler still, though less elegant, is to push four bamboo canes in the ground, slip the whole rubble sack over them, stake the bottom of the sack secure against the wind (and never mind that your garden has now become a billboard for Bloggs Building Supplies...)

 A Tip: stick an empty snail shell or cork on the end of each cane, or tie over it a piece of rubber cut from an old inner tube, or... the cane's sharp end will tear through the plastic in no time.

5. Cheesecloth cloches

To give seedlings sanctuary against driving wind and rain, make a micro-cloche quickly using a long strip of muslin or old netcloth curtain (from a charity shop) draped over wire hurdles and held down with soil or rocks. One wire clothes hanger will yield two hurdles.

Such cloches admit adequate light and water, and you can watch plants growing through the curtain until the time they bulge out the curtain and you can remove it. They do tend to blanch the leaves somewhat but this is a virtue, if you grow dandelions, endive or chicory. Blanching sweetens the leaves.

6. 'Bell jar' cloches

No coffee table gardening book today is deemed saleable unless it pictures a potager sporting a Victorian bell jar cloche.

> What few people know is that Victorian head gardeners *hated* them. Why? They first had to knock off that dratted round ball at the top. It acted like a magnifying glass, frying the plants...

You'll need a second mortgage to buy a bell jar today, however, so here's a cheaper idea. (It's free.)

Obtain some 22-litre plastic water reservoirs from an office water dispenser company. It must discard them after six uses, anyway, so should charge you nothing for the old empties. Saw the neck-end off, and the base - and you have a beautiful bell jar.

Pushed well into the soil, it's heavy enough to hold its own against all but a strong wind, and keeps out *everything*.

7. Bottle Bed cloches

If you've made **Bottle Beds *qv*,** you'll see how readily they can be turned into a cloche by encasing the entire structure in a large clear plastic bag, its ends tucked underneath.

> That gives seedlings total protection against everything but damping off disease. (A few ventilation holes should minimise that.)

As the plants grow, make the cloche taller by inserting short canes in four of the bottles. Cut increasing larger holes in the side of the bag to harden off the plants for a few days before removing the bag.

8. Other cloche ideas

Small clear containers like cola bottle halves and jam jars, of course, will protect single seedlings. *But beware!* A little plastic bottle cloche will fry your seedlings in moments, in a hot day. I once lost several precious plants that way. (So on a hot day, remove the cloche till nighttime...)

Large lampshades with metal frames can often be found cheaply at charity shops and car boot sales. Remove the fabric and replace with strong clear plastic.

Aquatic supply firms and stores often have broken aquariums. The hazardous glass can be replaced with perspex offcuts or clear rubble bag plastic.

> One ingenious allotment gardener even half-buried two bicycle wheels six foot apart and stretched plastic over them to form a tunnel cloche.

A large permanent cloche...

or rather low polytunnel, can be made using one inch pvc plumbing pipe.

This is bent into hoops, by softening the pipe in hot water, and the ends are pushed over rebars - metal pipes buried deeply in the ground. The frame is covered in robust clear horticultural plastic so the cloche should last two or three years.

It's best to build this cloche over a raised bed with wooden sides, so the plastic can be battened against the wood and easily raised when necessary for watering, plant access or temperature control (the interior can fluctuate between 10oC and 40oC over 24 hours in Spring).

The plastic can be removed in Summer, then replaced in Autumn to grow cold-weather crops like brassica throughout the Winter.

A permanent cloche like this could be built with a leaky pipe watering system buried just below the soil surface so it needs minimal maintenance.

The plastic would need to be battened very closely to the wooden frame, however, and the frame made gap-free - if molluscs are a problem.

Cloches are very versatile

Cloches are a simple way to extend your growing season, protect seedlings and transplants from every type of unfavourable environment, and best of all - by using ingenuity, they're free.

> *My favourite cloche...* is an old guinea pig run with clear plastic sheet tacked onto its wire net sides. In Summer, when it's not needed as a cloche, I take off the plastic, turn it vertically on its end, fill its base with compost - and grow tomatoes in it. The wire net then provides sturdy support for big Abraham Lincoln beefsteak tomatoes.
>
> In Autumn, I lay it back horizontally, put back the plastic, plant Winter lettuce transplants under it and... next year, start all over again.

* I've *never* seen a yeti in my garden. This proves my case, that cloches repel yetis.

How to grow *84* plants (you choose them) in just *2* square Foot or less

using Grow Poles and Grow Walls

> *"Build your castles in the air... then put foundations beneath them,"* H D Thoreau

If your garden is no larger than your kitchen (and you don't even have a kitchen), despair not. You hold or rent the freehold on an almost limitless growing area - the air above your head.

While there may be practical limits on exploiting your property to the full (veggie beds hanging from a tethered blimp may need permission from air traffic control), few of us make even modest use of our *vertical* growing spaces.

Weaving runner beans up canes or a bamboo trellis is no real challenge for the curly-minded gardener. Why not instead stake two sides from a child's **playpen** on top of each other? *Or* tip the frame from an old **bedstead** on its end, and support it upright like a Boy Scout tent?

> Painted pink and enhanced by Painted Lady bean florets, it becomes an *objet d'art* worthy of the Tate...

Let's get serious

Seriously, you might mount a bicycle wheel, hub cap, dustbin lid or the spokes of an old umbrella on a pole, with strings fanning from the rim.

Even make a raised bed using three old car tyres stacked on top of each other and tied together. Insert a pole in the middle, its lower end held firm with eg. a hollow breeze block. Fill the tyre bed with compost-rich soil. The strings can be tethered to the top tyre rim.

That way, you can grow runner beans even on a concrete patio... provided you keep the soil very well fed and watered as the plants develop.

Or stack six wooden coat hangers on top of each other, threaded centrally on a metal rod and with wires leading from their tips to the soil. That lets you grow 12 beans in little more than one square foot of ground.

Looking prettily like a microwave antenna, it suggests to your neighbours that you work for MI6 and will improve your credit rating.

Some hangers even have little notches at the end, making it easy to tie the strings.

Have you considered how wasteful of space are wigwams

ie. two rows of canes supporting a single cane at the top?

At least, plant some catchcrops within the wigwam meanwhile, to serve as ground cover and suppress weeds - such as radishes that will mature before the beans grow too big or lettuces (they'll grow even in deep shade).

Or a green manure that, when the beans shadow it, will die away gracefully - and add its nitrogen to the soil.

Even better, erect a tipi with the canes tied together in the *middle*. Then if you train them as they grow, the bean

 tips won't mat together in a muddle at the top and it's far easier to pick the beans, as they hang within hands' reach.

A Ziggurat grows 20% more plants

Given a few moments' work with a handsaw, you could make **Bean Ziggurats** that - in the same ground area - will grow 20% more beans than a conventional wigwam. Cut a sheet of 1/2 inch board into an octagon, each of the eight sides being six inches long. Drill holes at each corner. You now have an eight-sided board with eight holes.

Securely screw or nail that board to the top of a robust wooden stake - say, 2in square by 8 foot long - or a one inch metal pipe, and hammer the stake at least 18 inches into the ground.

Drop strings or wires vertically from each hole and tie them to sticks embedded in the soil.

It can be demonstrated that a 10 foot long wigwam supporting two rows of beans at 6inch intervals will grow 40 plants.

But the same ground area will permit six Bean Ziggurats, growing 48 plants.

That's because the Ziggurat design makes use of space *between* the rows that would otherwise be wasted.

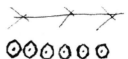

Climbing beans can tolerate some shade, especially at the roots. Provided the row of Ziggurats is aligned North-South, all plants will still get adequate light.

Leaning frames help cucurbits and ramblers

Give a gourd, pumpkin, melon, cucumber - or even a runner bean - enough food, water and light (and, of course, warmth) and they will ramble over half your allotment. But they will yield more produce in far less space, with less risk of rot or pest damage, if supported on a **frame**.

An old mattress base stripped of cloth, or a wooden pallet, or a wire bed frame, propped at a 45o angle facing south or west, provide fast if ugly support - and shade-tolerant plants like brassica can be grown in the shelter of the other side as well. So no ground is wasted.

Did you know, climbing beans don't *have* to climb? Just let them sprawl over a low frame. *Or do without a frame.* Pinch out their growing tip, and even runner beans will form big bushy plants without any staking at all. You just won't get as many beans.

A tip: cover a bare patch and suppress weeds temporarily by planting runner beans thickly, at six inch intervals both ways. *Without supports.* Coil them in circles. Then delight as they grow into a lush flower-rich edible jungle - and suppress *everything.*

You can even stir-fry and eat the growing tips of any beans - runner, french and broad beans. Just as you can the tops of pea plants. Yummy! *Another Yeoman breakthrough?*

More aesthetically, construct a robust wooden frame raised 18 inches above ground and top it with 4 or 6-inch poultry netting. That will also support cordon tomatoes or broad beans or (if you *must* grow non-edible flowers) carnations as well.

Any smaller mesh, and you won't get your hands in to pluck the produce. That frame had better also be strong - a dozen beefsteak tomato plants in full fruit weigh even more than I do. And that's a *lot.*

If you design your frame cleverly, it can double as a cold frame in Spring (simply make detachable wooden sides that can be bolted on to complete a box when needed). And also as a mini-polytunnel to grow lettuce and cabbage all Winter.

Another idea: construct *two* tops, framed respectively in wire netting for Summer and perspex or tough clear plastic for other times in the year, and alternate them through the seasons.

Grow your beans as a cordon, slant-ways

Bean tendrils on a wigwam or tipi can easily rise eight foot or more, blocking your neighbours' view and becoming vulnerable to gales. The wind pressure on a fully grown wigwam is strong enough to drive a small yacht at a fast rate of knots (or, if you have Force 8 gales as I do, to propel it to Mach 1).

> So why not borrow a trick from apple and pear growers, and train climbing french and pole beans to grow *at an angle* - cordon-style?

When I had 11 climbing french bean transplants to stake, but nowhere to stake them, I mounted an 8-foot bamboo cane horizontally atop three 4-foot cane uprights. Then I fanned 11 strings from the horizontal cane at 8 inch intervals, diagonally downward to the left and right, and staked the ends of the string in the ground alongside the beans.

I constructed this cordon against my neighbour's short (4 foot) fence, using only a negligible amount of ground area, and it was almost invisible from his side. But from my side, the flowery view was spectacular. As was the produce.

Moral: climbing beans - and tomatoes, pumpkins, melons and cucumbers - *can* be trained, like fruit trees and grapes, to grow at an angle. *Even around corners.*

Or *from* your garden and, though a convenient hole, *into* your greenhouse or polytunnel (so you don't have to water them so often). All using minimal space!

Disguise garden eyesores

Of course, climbing beans, squashes and gourds have long been used as decorative shields for eyesores like oil tanks, lawn rollers, privies, sheds, decayed loggias and benches, wood and junk piles, statues in questionable taste, compost heaps, dad's bicycle, dad himself, old ladders, rusted childrens' swings and the like.

A tip: if you haven't already shredded last year's Christmas tree, stick it in the ground and train beans up it...

After all, runner beans were until the 19th century grown for their decorative flowers alone, as textbook authors tirelessly remind us.

Even a small tub in the patio or yard or by the porch should, if well fed, grow enough beans or small squashes to decorate a wall or hide an ugly view - though such cramped plants will not fill your freezer.

Tip: if you erect a new floral arch or arbour with a view to growing roses, clematis, honeysuckle and the like, there's no need to wait three years or more for an abundant show of colour.

Plant climbing beans among those perennials *now* - and enjoy the flowers *this* season!

Idea: You could mix climbing nasturtiums in with the beans and eat the nasturtium flowers and luscious spicey leaves too...

Create a Grow Pole

No garden at all? Well, if you have just a yard or patio or *any* outside area with reasonable light on most sides, you can grow 24 lettuces - or almost any small plant - in less than one square foot of ground area.

You need just a six-inch plastic gutter or sewer pipe, 7 foot in length, and 12 empty 4 pint or 2-litre plastic milk cartons.

Sink the bottom of the pipe one foot in the ground and cement it in. If that's not possible, you'll need to construct a firm base on the flat ground, somewhat like a Xmas tree support, to hold the pipe securely upright. (In that case, your pipe need be only six foot long.)

Drill two holes in the pipe one foot up from the ground, each hole being on either side of the pipe. Drill a similar set of two holes, six inches further on. Then drill a similar set one foot

further long, then another six inches further on... and so on.

These holes will allow you to thread plasticated string or, better, nylon sash cord or washing line, through the pipe to support bandoliers of growing containers, made from the milk cartons.

Cut the milk cartons in half, keeping the caps screwed on, so you have 24 open tubs. Drill several perforations in the base for drainage plus four holes in the sides at the back, two at the bottom and two at the top.

Now loop six of the tubs into a bandolier by threading cord through first the lower holes then the upper holes. (A big darning needle makes this easy, or a 'needle' can be contrived from stiff wire with a flat loop at one end.) Lash those bandoliers around the pipe at one foot intervals, using the holes in the pipe to secure them.

Beware: don't use wire to secure the cartons as wire will cut into the jugs' plastic. It's actually easier to fix the bandoliers (I find) if you secure them together three at a time, not six, and band them to one side of the pipe. Then fix the remaining three to the other side.

Fill the cartons with a lightweight mix of vermiculite, water retentive granules and compost (mixed with peat, if you're not environmentally sensitive, or with dried moss scraped off your roof, if you are), plus an inch of polybeads at the base to help drainage.

Remember: when wet, those cartons will be heavy.

And plant in them lettuce transplants. Or herbs. Or cherry tomatoes. Or strawberries. Even flowers.

If unattended, that Grow Pole will quickly dry out and exhaust its nutrients so water and feed it regularly, using a soluble organic feed like nettle or comfrey tea.

Yes, it *is* fiddly to set up a Grow Pole the first year. (It took me all of three hours, once I had the materials to hand, and most of that was spent making the wooden base support.)

But it's an investment.

You could readily grow as many 72 lettuces successively from April to September, far more than most families can eat - especially if you grow the 'cut and come again' kind. Or a wealth of cherry tomatoes. Or more parsley than is needed for a Rotarians' banquet (that's a *lot* of parsley).

The cartons can be emptied and washed in a weak bleach solution in Autumn, then stored for re-use next Spring, and the next. They last for years, accidents apart, and can easily be replaced at no cost when necessary.

Put your Grow Pole in your yard

If you're lucky enough to have a warm reflecting South-facing wall or a favoured micro-climate eg. by your central heating vent, or a sheltered yard eg. under a car porch, your Grow Pole positioned there could continue to yield you greens like...

lettuce, sorrel, Chinese cabbage, land cress, corn salad and the like all Winter long... especially if you position shiney foil, a mirror or mirror plastic at the pole's darkest side to reflect back the available light.

Tip: cut the sides out of cola cans and tack them, interior side outward, to a board. It gives a wondrously shiny mirror.

That's useful in Winter, especially if you grow plants in your conservatory, greenhouse or on a window sill. Put the 'mirror' behind the plants, to reflect back the daylight.

Frost aside, it's *not* low temperatures that stop temperate-zone crops from growing in Winter. *Mostly, it's the lack of light!*

On frosty or windy Winter days, slip a protective shroud of perforated clear plastic, fleece or muslin over the pole. Even if the lettuces freeze solid, they'll miraculously revive when the air thaws. Lettuces have elastic cell walls.

Above all, add more breeze blocks to the base support!

Now... for the truly curly-minded: a Grow Wall

Like to grow as many as 84 lettuces or other small edible plants in just 2 sq ft of ground area? No problem. Just erect a **Grow Wall.**

Do you have an outdoor surface that receives adequate sunlight, and preferably South or West-facing, that's at least 4ft by 6ft? It could be your house wall (of course) or else your fence, garage, oil tank, shed, terrace or verandah - even, in a block of flats, the surfaces adjacent to your lightest window.

That's your **Grow Wall**. Let me explain...

We've already seen that one plastic milk jug can be cut in half to make two good grow pots. Suppose you acquired 42 plastic jugs, cut them into 84 half-pots, and stapled them to a wooden frame 4ft wide by 6ft tall?

You could erect that against any outside surface, given reasonable light, and it would grow year-round more small edible plants or herbs than you could ever eat and in just 2 sq ft of ground area.

> In fact, if lifted off the ground and screwed to the wall it would need, strictly speaking, no land whatever.

Here's step-by-step how to do it

Assuming your jugs are like mine around 4 inches wide, 6 inches deep and 11 inches tall:

Cut the jugs in half. Cut off the corners at the base, or perforate the neck sides, for drainage. Drill 1/4 inch holes at either side, in the 6 inch walls, at the back and around 1 inch below the top. This is where you thread the supporting wire or string.

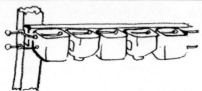

Make a simple wooden frame using 7 lathes 4ft long by about 4 inches deep and 1/2 inch thick, screwed on top of two similar lathe 6 ft tall.

It's wise to use thicker wood for these upright supports, however, and to add a third support in the middle. When the pots are wet, they'll be bearing a lot of weight.

Hammer 1/2 inch metal staples along each horizontal lathe, 4 inches apart and 1 inch from the top. Then use washing line or nylon sash cord to thread the half-jugs onto the lathes, inserting it into the staples as you go. Tie it securely to the staples at both ends.

Note: stiff washing line is impossible to tie securely so, to hold it taut, loop the line back over the last staple and lash it with wire. Thin plasticated string is not recommended to support the jugs as it tears through the holes.

Do the same for all the horizontal lathes. Put a layer of expanded polystyrene pieces at the bottom of each pot, and fill with a lightweight porous mixture of compost and vermiculite or perlite. Sand is cheaper than vermiculite, but useless here: it's too heavy for the plastic.

So if you're penurious, aerate the compost with finely shredded fragments of polystyrene - though it's hardly an organic option. Or smash up lots of snail shells.

You now have a Grow Wall!

True, it's somewhat ugly, especially if the milk labels are still visible. So paint the jugs in a motley of colours or, more easily, clad them in black plastic strips affixed at each end with thumb tacks.

If you're *truly* curly-minded, your imagination will already be leaping in the direction of a **Grow Mural**.

For vibrant colour, plant annual flowers at random intervals - then replace them with Winter lettuces and the like in Autumn.

Leave gaps between some pots at each level, set climbing plants in a few lower pots, and let them snake their way upwards through the gaps.

With 84 pots, you have ample space to be creative!

Indeed, why have all your pots the same size or at the same level?

Jugs can be cut into different depths and set at different positions below or above the line, and filled with a well-composed balance of plants and flowers both big and small.

You'll have a living wall relief worthy of Mondrian or Le Corbusier. And so beauteous will it be, in its minimalist elegance, that you can exhibit it at the Chelsea Flower Show and become famous.

If your Grow Mural happens also to feed you, year round, that's then a bonus...

I confess... While I did (truly) make a wondrous Grow Wall, I never did go on to make a Grow Mural. I hate fame.

GROW ANYTHING IN ANYTHING (WELL, ALMOST)

In praise of old laundry baskets

There's an unpronounceable Japanese saying much quoted in the martial arts that means, in effect, *'use all available weapons'*.

Much joy did I once have watching a tiny female karate ace dispatch, in a lurid video, a thug - not with her hands - but with the lid of a garbage can.

> 'Why do things the hard way, by hand, if easier means are, uh, to hand?' was the message.

We can use the same principle in gardening. Almost any discarded item we have around the house or yard can be recycled to save money, grow or shield plants, or entertain the neighbours.

For example, I'd have used that garbage can more fruitfully to...

grow potatoes, make compost, brew fertiliser 'tea', breed worms or incinerate wood into fertilising ash. The lid might have provided a bird bath, purslane or watercress bed or - with strings fanning from it - have grown beans or supported tomatoes.

Look out for scrap - it's profit for you!

When a relative refurbished her kitchen, I inherited no less than:

- an emporium of drawers for **seed trays**,
- formica surfaces for the bases of **hydroponic beds**,
- a refrigerator full of plastic trays for **Grow Beds**,
- glass shelves for **cold frames** and wire racks to put over the Aga to **dehydrate** vegetables (I even sank the case in the soil and covered it with straw as a **root cellar**),
- a fridge-freezer, wherein I put my juiced tomatoes (top freezer unit) and my heirloom seeds for long-term **storage** (bottom fridge unit),
- a metal sink to act as a water reservoir for an automatic **seed sprouter**,
- a plethora of old washing up bowls and laundry baskets for **Grow Trays**,
- empty plastic detergent bottles to cut up into plant **labels** and **ties**,
- *plus* lumber, screws and metal fittings galore for every purpose.

Only television 'gardeners' claim that *any* old junk can be associated with growing plants and, at once, it becomes picturesque. (I suspect a toilet bowl will always be an aesthetic challenge, even if it overflows with cherry tomatoes.)

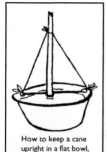

How to keep a cane upright in a flat bowl, using strings at each four angles

And too many old tyres strewn around your backyard could give organic gardening (and you) a bad name.

But you should rarely have to pay high prices at a garden centre, if you use your imagination.

With beer cans, wine bottles, old laundry baskets, wash basins, plastic milk jugs and the like freely to hand you need never buy another plant pot, or other gardening hardware, ever again.

But how about these further ideas?

• Are you infested with couch grass, nettles or bindweed?

Rejoice! If your soil is a mattress of couchgrass or similar roots, impossible to remove, be happy. Wash and chop those fat white succulent roots, and mix them in with your next stir fry and *eat* them! Highly nutritious (truly).

You have a perpetual vegetable supply...

Or loop the cut roots around the tendrils of growing runner beans, clematis, honeysuckle, cucumbers, or other climbing plants to secure them to their canes or strings.

 A tip: as every Victorian gardener knew, fibrous weed roots, grass or bindweed tendrils are a useful handy twine!

By the time the weed roots rot off (now too dry to be a menace), the bean tendrils &c will have found their new path.

• Substitute sharp builder's sand for costly vermiculite or perlite.

If you must buy sand, to ensure good drainage when making potting mixtures, go to a builder's merchant or trade warehouse like B&Q where 25 kgms will cost around £1 - as opposed to £5 at the garden shop.

• **Use wood chip or cocoa husks...**

as grow beds for ring culture or hydroponics, instead of expanded clay pellets or vermiculite. They're light enough to sit on greenhouse racking even when wet and, though costly to buy, can be used next season as a mulch.

 Beware: wood chip or cocoa husks are slightly acidic, with a pH around 5.4, so add some wood ash or lime to them.

• **Acquire several builder's ballast sacks from a development site...**

These are the giant plastic indestructible kind that can lift tons of sand. They're free, because builders (nowadays) fecklessly throw them away after one use.

Slash them with holes to make... compost bins *or* grow potatoes, *or* turn down the sides to make instant raised beds, *or* put vexatious kiddies in them (an instant play pen), *or* use them like a wheelbarrow to collect leaves and grass clippings, *or* drag them behind you as you weed your beds - lying on your back (as you should)...

• **Grow plants in shopping bags**

Almost any small to medium-sized plant can be grown in a plastic shopping bag, perforated at the bottom, filled with compost and loosely tied at the top.

Unlike commercial grow bags, they're small enough to slip in anywhere - eg. at the end of paths - and flexible enough to squeeze into bare spaces between plants or pots.

Hang one on each side of a fence, like a saddle bag.

> **A Tip:** Supermarket bags rot away in weeks under sunlight. So use only tough plastic bags, like the kinds from posh shops and off-licences. Imagine... a *Fortnum & Mason* grow wall!

• Forget about hiring a costly shredder to turn twigs into mulch.

Lay them on a well-trimmed lawn or flat surface and use a sturdy rotary lawnmower to shred them.

• Grow your own 'bamboo' canes free, to stake next year's beans or tomatoes - from giant sunflowers.

Or cherish the canes from Jerusalem artichokes. They're fragile, but will furnish you pea, bean or tomato supports for at least another year.

Cut elder or hazel branches in Autumn, when they have to be trimmed anyway.

All make far more decorative bean and tomato tipis than do bamboos, and they'll last longer than you think, if you overwinter them every year in your garage.

> **Beware:** elder branches I cut in *Spring* blossomed exultantly into new leaf, when I planted them as bean poles.

Carrots and onions growing well in old laundry baskets

Idea: use Spring-cut branches to grow a fast leafy yurt or bower, a playhouse for your children (or you)!

• **Explore the potential of old castaways...**

Such as wellies or hiking boots, wheelbarrows, kayaks, watering cans, washing up bowls, hollowed logs and dog baskets. Use them as grow pots.

An old bathtub is deep enough to grow almost anything and can look like a priceless Victorian lead trough if you paint the outside grey then paint it lavishly with yogurt or manure water.

Or just mix fresh horse or cow dung with clay and smear it on by hand.

> Young children love doing this, I find, provided you assure them it's dirty, an EC hygiene directive has forbidden it, and so they *mustn't*.

This technique produces ancient-looking mould and lichens, almost instantly. So while you're about it, it's worth doing it on every other ugly permanent feature in your garden as well. Dad's bicycle comes up a treat...

• **Ugly containers can be disguised by coating them with hypertufa.**

Mix equal parts of cement, shredded peat moss or (if you dislike using peat moss) dried leaves, and sharp builder's sand - plus just enough water so you can mould it. Arrange a frame round your pot with chicken wire and thickly slap on the gruel.

Or make an impermeable frame around the pot with plastic sheet, using corks below the pot to raise it above the lower sheet. Then pour the gruel in.

> After a day or two, remove the plastic and 'age' the surface with deft chisel marks, if you wish. Leave it for six weeks out of the rain to dry thoroughly before you plant in it.

Mock boulders and garden gargoyles can, I'm told, be made the same way. If you make the insides hollow, your hypertufa (whoever invented that silly name?) will go a lot further.

> **Beware:** Hypertufa is so porous, plants will actually root into it. So it *won't* make you a waterproof garden pool.

• Make an impromptu cold frame.

Any wily gardener can make a cold frame using bricks and an old window, free. A millionaire would instead buy some aluminium 'cold frame' from a garden centre that is guaranteed to break down within 12 months.

But here's a cheaper way that...

> *also helps build you a highly fertile garden to last out the rest of your years.*

In Spring, stack up bales of **newspaper** for the sides, and top them with corrugated clear plastic held down with bricks.

> Tightly bound newspaper bales resist rain far longer than you'd think. Tie them with degradeable twine then *everything* rots down eventually, by next year if you're lucky.

In Summer, fill the interior with topsoil and compost to make a raised bed and in Autumn mix the now-rotted newspaper into the heap along with - ideally - some extra manure. Next Spring, you'll have a richly fertile plot.

 A Tip: you can do that *anywhere*, even on a concrete base.

• **Collect large clear plastic bags from dry cleaners.**

A double thickness of this plastic makes a 'quick fix' cloche, if well tethered. So do those pestilential giant plastic bags that surround new kitchen appliances. Each is big enough to yield you a modest *polytunnel*.

• **Hoard expanded polystyrene...**

the unwelcome kind that manufacturers put into household appliance cartons (and which is so vexatious to get rid of).

Break it into chunks to layer the bottoms of your plant pots. Polybeads are especially good. Half fill a large pot with these plastic fragments and you'll need much less compost. Wash them in mild bleach every year and you can re-use them indefinitely,

Tip: put an upturned flower pot at the bottom of a large container - or lay several across the bottom of a big tray. It has the same effect and halves the compost you need.

Another idea: I've had great results using a variation on **ring culture** in the greenhouse to grow tomatoes.

I obtained several large plastic storage boxes from a diy shed at a knock-down price, and drilled drainage holes in the bottoms. I put eight small plastic flower pots in the containers, *upside down*. Then I filled the storage boxes with a mix of home-made compost, topsoil and sand.

On top of the soil I set two large 9-inch plastic flowerpots, with their bases cut out, and turned upside down.

In those elevated pots, I grew my tomatoes. In October when the tomatoes died back, I removed them and scattered the contents of the top pots over the trays - then set in cabbage transplants intercropped with land cress seedlings.

(I might also - I suppose - have grown many kinds of Winter-tolerant Chinese brassica. But I didn't. Because, frankly, I find they don't taste very nice.)

I found these plants cropped continually, if slowly, even though January temperatures in my unheated greenhouse dropped frequently below zero.

• Make edible plants go far further.

Did you know...

~ you can pinch off tomato 'suckers', the extraneous shoots that grow between the main stems, and insert them in a pot of compost early in the season to create a new plant?

Surround them with a polybag cloche supported on twigs for the first few weeks and keep them *very* well watered.

~ Trim and eat the outer leaves from brassica and lettuces as they grow and you will get up to eight times the yield than if you simply cut the mature plant?

~ If you crop a cabbage or any other brassica, and cut a cross in the top of the stem, edible new leaves will grow?

~ If you let a cabbage (well, *some* cabbages) go to seed, a tough stalk will emerge as high as six foot or more - which you can then dry to use as a bean support next year. Or a walking stick?

~ The tough stems of giant sunflowers or Jerusalem artichokes can be dried, cut into one foot lengths, lashed together with plasticated string and unrolled as temporary *pathways* through your garden beds?

Quite apart from their uses as bean & tomato tripods, lawn edgings, yurt supports and fierce-burning logs for your grate.

~ When thinning seedlings, you can eat the thinnings in salads or chop them into a casserole or stir fry.

Almost all vegetable thinnings and growing tops are edible - with the important exception of tomatoes, rhubarb and potatoes.

~ If radishes go to seed, eat the seed capsules in stir fries or salads - spicily delicious!

Forgive me, if you're truly a curly-minded gardener. *I know* you learned those ideas years ago (when I was just a seedling)...

• Save all the seeds you can at end of the season...

For example, tie a piece of panty hose or nylon sock around the drying seed head to deter birds and retain the seeds.

If they're not from hybrid plants (F1 or F2), they'll grow you another good crop next year.

Or just sprinkle them in any unemployed place anyway, and see what delightful folly comes up..

• Make your own onion sets!

Grow a seedbed - or a deep trayful - of onions from seed, sowing them thickly, *but don't thin them.* You'll get a mass of tiny onion bulbs that won't develop.

In Autumn, ease them gently out of the soil with a kitchen fork, leaving their root tips still in the soil. Leave them lying for a week or so on top of the soil.

Then pull them, trim the roots off and store them in a dry cool place. Next Spring, plant them out.

And here's a tip you've never read elsewhere: One year I planted a bed of onion sets but, when weeds overgrew them, I forgot about them. In late Autumn when the weeds died back I noticed the onions were still alive, though meagre, so I stored the bulbs. Next Spring I planted them out and - yes, they all went to seed as they should, being biennials.

So I cut off those tall elegant seed stalks and ate them as spring onions. (They also lasted for weeks - and looked beautiful - kept on the kitchen window sill in a vase.)

The roots then grew into big plump onions, as if it was their very first year, and we stored them trussed in plaits. *Two crops in one!*

True, seed saving is a deep and complex science. For example, if you want your seeds to grow true next year you should have grown them far away from others of the same species, last year. Some species are more tolerant than others.

You can safely grow runner and french climbing beans together, I've found, and they won't cross-pollinate. But different kinds of brassica or lettuce need to be kept at least a *mile* apart! Or their seeds next year will grow aberrantly - and somewhat peculiarly.

Kept in a refrigerator in a sealed jar with dessicant gel or dried milk powder to reduce moisture, most seeds will last *at least* another two years or more.

Even parsnips will, *whatever* the textbooks say. I'm currently growing parsnip seeds I stored three years ago, though they're supposed to be good in storage for just one year.

Some seeds like pumpkins, cucumbers and other cucurbits may stay viable for ten years or more.

• **An easy way to store seeds.**

I just dry them on kitchen paper at room temperature, then store them in seal-top jars in the fridge.

I don't bother to sort glutinous seeds like tomatoes individually or to 'ferment' them in water as some textbooks advise. Life is too short.

Just scrape the jelly-like seeds onto kitchen paper, let it dry at room temperature, then store the paper - with the seeds stuck to it. Fragments can later be cut out and planted, paper and all.

> *It works,* as my 100 heirloom tomato plants now pollulating outside - and all grown from my own seed last year - will attest!

• Don't waste any surplus seeds...

even if you *don't* intend to plant them, like those from hybrid plants which may not grow anything worthwhile next year.

> *Though, who knows?* A hairy, yellow & pink striped melon, the result of growing a saved F1 seed, may fit no catalogue description... but why not sample it anyway?

Otherwise questionable seeds saved from hybrid cultivars can still be **Sprouted *qv*** then stir-fried, juiced or eaten in salads (with obvious exceptions like tomatoes, potatoes and rhubarb, as we've seen.)

• The proof of the planting

Just to show that it's a *wonderful* idea to use any old container - and that these planting ideas work - I've graciously included some candid photos from my garden overleaf, to prove it...

Honest, they looked lovely in colour - but then, hm, don't *all* vegetables look grey in the dark?

Parsnips growing healthily in loo rolls in a plastic tub, just 2 inches apart!

Carrots transplanted using loo rolls and growing - several 2 inches wide - in a laundry basket

Courgettes pollulating out of an old sink, and threatening to overrun the garden

YOG - *THE ULTIMATE ORGANIC MULCH*

Introducing Yeoman's Organic Glop...

Ever needed to mulch a new vegetable or flower bed to suppress weeds before you set out plants or seedlings?

You've plenty of options but most are unsightly, expensive or unobtainable - especially in towns. For example:

Cocoa shells or wood bark are decorative but cost a pop star's ransom. Pea gravel likewise, and once it's there - it's there forever. Forget about ever growing prize carrots or parsnips in that soil.

> **A Tip:** You could always dig a two-foot post hole and fill it with a mix of sand and sifted topsoil, of course, for every tuber you plant. I assume you'd rather not do that, so I'll proceed....

Not everyone has lavish quantities of compost, rotted straw, dead leaves or sawdust freely to hand (though in Autumn your council's park maintenance dept may provide leaves or a National Trust office may deliver you trailer loads of cut bracken, free, as it once did for me).

Away with old newspapers...

Black polythene is neither environmentally friendly nor attractive, unless you cover it with other mulch (better make lots of slits to let in the rain unless you use the permeable kind, which is costly). Old newspapers and cardboard are free but even more ugly. And if you're me, newspapers tend to protract the planting process. (I keep stopping to read the headlines.)

Moreover, they blow everywhere unless held down with muck, bricks, planks or soil-filled plastic bags. So very soon your beloved garden looks like a tinker's yard.

Wouldn't it be useful to have the equivalent of permeable plastic fleece, that's totally organic, biodegradeable, enriches the soil, repels slugs and snails, is simple to make, looks good - and costs virtually nothing?

I knew you'd agree, so here it is:

Yeoman's Organic Glop.

Jest not. I've used it successfully on flower and vegetable beds and, though it *does* take a smidgen of preparation, it's far less work than humping gravel or wrestling with plastic in a high wind. All of which I've done, as my aching back will testify.

First, collect a 3ft stack of old newspapers. That's one month's supply, in my house, though you could get endless quantities from neighbours - if you promise *not* to offer them your surplus courgettes come Summer.

Beware: Discard glossy magazines. Newspaper ink - either black or colour - is usually carbon-based nowadays and safe for vegetable growing, but glossies may still use toxic inks.

Second, procure a waterproof dustbin, wheelie bin, old sink, pond liner or plastic builder's sack. I was lucky to have a derelict shower pedestal to hand. Put that empty container at the end of your plot now - because, unless it's a wheelie bin, you won't be able to move it when it's full.

Now wait until a time when the ground's wet but the weather's dry. If your soil is dry, soak it lavishly.

> **Important note:** I assume your soil is in good heart, neither too acid nor too alkaline - with a pH ideally between 6 and 7, fertile, reasonably friable and it has no serious rocks, mineral deficiencies, pollution or perennial weeds.

> Glop will suppress even couchweed and dock for a season but, unless you get their roots out now, they'll come back next season - glop or not.

> **A Tip:** To kill almost any perennial weed, lop them off at ground level then pour a large heap of salt on the remaining stems. It really works, for tuberous dock, dandelion and thistles, at least. But, overdone, it devastates your soil...

Make sure you've hoed off all annual weeds first. It makes it easier to lay the glop.

Third, using a hose, fill the container with water. Add wallpaper paste, in the quantities suggested on the package for very light use.

Wallpaper paste is curiously strong

In fact, you can get away with diluting the paste three-fold, and still it will work: modern paste is very strong. Four gallons of well diluted paste should handle 400 sq ft of ground.

Okay, you have to buy that paste but, if you visit a builders supply merchant, you can get bulk packs at silly low prices. I'm talking around £5 to handle 400 sq ft of ground, if you're economical with the paste, dilute it well and squeeze it thoroughly out of the glop before laying it. Compare that with the price of mulching with permeable black plastic!

Please don't ask me the metric equivalent: I'm proudly British.

Purists might substitute flour for commercial wallpaper paste. Flour paste was a proven glue before wallpaper paste went on the market, and is much cheaper. But I haven't tested it.

Standard wallpaper paste should contain no chemicals that can harm your plants. Indeed, I have seen it recommended that small or just-sprouted seeds be mixed with made-up wallpaper paste so they can be extruded from a tube for easier planting.

Fourth, lay your newspaper in that paste, some eight or more pages thick, in succession so that all is totally saturated. It's easier to handle the newspaper if you fold it to tabloid - the size of scurrilous newspapers. Leave to soak overnight.

Fifth, totally squeeze out all excess paste - while keeping the paper flat - by pressing against the container side.

Your glop is ready!

Lay it over the ground approx one quarter inch thick, or - if you have a big perennial weed problem like me - a half-inch thick. Overlap each edge by three inches, press firmly together and into the soil, and pray the weather stays dry for 48 hours. A few light showers won't stop the glop drying but, if a thunderstorm is threatened, protect it with old compost bags or plastic sheet.

You can lay YOG in moments

"It's going to rain!" my wife lamented. "Don't worry," I assured her. "I've covered the glop with plastic." She glowered "I was thinking about my washing!"

Some women have no sense of priorities...

Result: after a few days of dry weather your glop (a sort of papier mache) should have moulded itself to the ground like a shell, elegant and beautiful. Did I hear you say 'oh, horticultural paper'? Wash your mouth out. That's like comparing Michelangelo with Andy Worhol...

No need to hold it down with unsightly bricks or mulch. It will resist wind, stop weeds dead for several months, and prevent slugs and snails creeping over the top or harbouring inside - then rot away gracefully in Autumn.

What's more, it can bring you many other benefits too...

Don't like its mottled grey appearance?

Mix lots of lawn clippings into the paste, or spread them on top, so your glop is (in the early days, at least) a fashionable textured green. This will rot the YOG faster - in three months, in my experience - but looks pretty meanwhile.

> When rotted it produces a superb compost, adding the high-nitrogen of grass to the high-carbon of paper.

Or colour it with childrens' powder paint (dark green or brown are best). It won't leach out. *Or* use a permanent, bio-friendly, dye. That's guaranteed to leave its souvenirs on your clothes, of course.

> One answer is to take your clothes off before laying YOG. But I'll reserve that discussion for the *Erotic Review*....

Or lay on straw, dried leaves, pine needles, whatever fine-chopped organic matter you have available - to give a textured glop that's far cheaper than wood bark.

You could also sprinkle sharp builders sand. While the glop is still wet, it sticks very nicely and creates your own sandpaper (for a while, at least) - which molluscs hate.

Or spread crushed eggshells or sea shells, smashed snail shells, even chopped teasel, blackberry stems or thistle leaves - anything having prickly edges - lavishly on top before the glop dries.

Result: you'll have some temporary protection against slugs and snails. This works especially in the early weeks when your seeds or transplants are most vulnerable, and before rain mitigates the deterrents' effect.

> I concede, when conditions are very wet - and slugs and snails are endemic - it seems nothing but a water moat will deter them.

Or mix into the glop green manure seeds. So when the glop rots, it will be replaced by an over-wintering blanket of nitrogenous field beans or clover...

What do you do with GLOP?

Everything! The delight of glop is that you can design your beds exactly as you want them. Plant what you wish, week by week, patch by patch - building as you grow. Safe from weeds.

Cut small holes in the glop and plant transplants. That hardened glop also saves you laying mats around brassica to deter soil-infesting moths and other pests - just put

back the same square you cut, with a slit to accommodate the stem.

Or cut the glop open in a cross-cross fashion, then lay it back. Laid around gooseberry and other berry bushes in Spring, glop also prevents over-wintering sawfly caterpillars from emerging.

Cut long narrow slits then plant seeds such as carrots, beetroot, parsnips and lettuce.

> But first, make a shallow trench in the slit and fill it with sterilised fine soil or sand. I find carrots are best sown *broadcast*-style in small square patches, thinning them as they grow, then tamping down the soil to avoid attracting carrot flies. Their lush growth suppresses all weeds.

Or plant edible beneficial flowers like nasturtiums (which repel aphids and seduce caterpillars away from your brassicas). *Or* aromatic herbs, which confuse pests.

Or tagetes or calendula (both are marigolds, by any other name). Not only can you eat marigold flowers and leaves, of course (and they're actually nicer than most lettuces), they also support the growth of virtually every plant and repel *everything*...

Dig shallow holes and plant onion sets, sunflowers, broad beans, french and runner beans - or even chitted potatoes. (You'll need to earth the potatoes up when the leaves appear eg. by tossing on straw. But there's no need to dig or make deep holes.)

Did I not mention flowers?

Of course, you can plant bulbs straight through holes in YOG, too.

Any large seeds, transplants or bulbs will enlarge their own path through holes in YOG as they grow. Meanwhile, the glop deters opportunistic weeds.

Of course, you'll never need YOG to grow jerusalem artichokes. Just toss them into any old soil. They'll grow to 12 foot and last forever, suppressing everything meanwhile and resisting all attempts to dig them out, and you can bequeath them to your children...

But I digress.

YOG is the most elegant answer to home garden mulching that I've found. Try it!

As Alexander Pope prettily wrote in his *'Tribute to YOG'* (1742):

> Greater joy, hath mankind never felt
> Than laying YOG, in verdant fertile belt.
> See what delights in sylvan scenes appear.
> Grub Street's waste creates - *Elysium* here!

True, Pope never thought to write that. But as I'm a better poet than Pope, and he was unacquainted with YOG, I pardon him.

'Drilling' seed - a new low-cost way

To plant small seeds in YOG, like carrots, lettuce or radish, I first drilled half-inch holes in it using - yes, forgive me - a cordless drill. Then I inserted purchased seed tapes, torn off at one inch intervals, spilled and thrust into the holes.

How to make your own seed tape

That worked so brilliantly, I went on to make my own **'seed tape'** - at a fraction the price!

Simply cover one sheet of newspaper or kitchen paper thinly with your left-over wallpaper paste. Sprinkle the

seed of your choice on it sparsely - about 3 seeds per square inch. Press on another sheet of newspaper and leave to dry overnight in an airing cupboard. Then cut it into one inch squares. (If you're laying strips, of course, cut it into strips).

Spill each square and push that spill into the little hole. Make sure the bottom of the spill is fully imbedded in the soil or your seedling will sprout but have nowhere to go. The newspaper rots away in no time and meanwhile its absorbency helps the seed to grow. As it grows, the seed muscles aside the YOG and grows to its full potential.

This sounds fiddly, but takes only moments to do. And it's far easier to make your own 'seed tape' indoors at your leisure than trying to drop individual seeds into little holes in the garden in a gale.

You could make all the seed tapes you need for a whole allotment, in under an hour, even if you *don't* use YOG. Lay them on the soil, sprinkle some fine sand or sterilised soil on top, and that's it.

Result: far less labour than cutting 'drills' then hand sowing and covering them.

It actually, truly works.

It gives a new meaning to the phrase 'drilling seeds'. And - if you use YOG - you can also plant out your plot like a Turkish carpet, and keep it weed-free, with micro-precision!

These lettuces catch-cropped with broccoli were literally 'drilled' into the YOG using a cordless drill. The holes were filled with spools of home-made seed tape, bedded one half-inch into the topsoil.

The Official YOG Technician's Uniform

If you add a tasteful non-toxic dye to your YOG, it will inevitably migrate onto your clothes and you will look like a Druid. If you lay YOG without wearing any clothes, the postman will think you're a naturist and people will talk.

To avoid either embarrassment, first slip on the **Official YOG Technician's Uniform.**

Discard all your clothes save sandals and shorts. Take a black plastic kitchen rubbish sack and cut arm holes on either side at the base plus a hole in the middle for your head. Slip it over your torso and use the ties that are often helpfully provided at the top of the sack to belt it around your waist.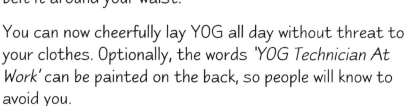

You can now cheerfully lay YOG all day without threat to your clothes. Optionally, the words '*YOG Technician At Work*' can be painted on the back, so people will know to avoid you.

Seriously, always keep a YOG Uniform to hand, folded in your car, bicycle pannier or garage, in the event of sudden rain, muck-shifting or chores that call for close contact with grease or paint.

It is also an excellent adjunct to kneading bread dough, hosing down the car or *dwyle flunking*.

The latter is an historic Bedfordshire sport, in which a ring of fun-loving villagers take turns throwing cow pats at some unfortunate in the middle, whose task is to avoid them. Today, the cow pats have been replaced by wet flannels. (And no, I am *not* making this up.)

YEOMAN'S LAZY SOD

How to make a high-yielding raised bed without the backache

The laziest 'no dig' style of gardening calls for just throwing kitchen scraps then spoiled hay or straw on the ground in Autumn and walking away.

Pile this midden high enough - two or three foot is best - and by Spring it will have rotted down to a fertile slightly raised bed. Scrape away the top muck, plant your transplants, then keep laying mulch to deter weeds.

> **Result:** you need never weed or dig again. Plus the curvature of the bed lets you grow 150% more plants, set more closely together than normal, and get a super-productive yield.

It sounds too good to be true, and it is.

Thick mulch is a paradise for slugs and snails and, if these are endemic in your garden (and aren't they everywhere?), you won't have a crop. Few urban homes have access to enough free straw/hay to build a *deep* muck sandwich. And to lay that volume of biomass in any sizeable garden, you'd need a tractor.

So it's nice for farmers but the rest of us can forget it.

At the other extreme is French intensive gardening where the bed is double dug every four years. In trials by the US magazine *Mother Earth News*, these beds were more productive after two years than 'no dig' beds. Even so, I doubt whether the extra food produced by double digging would ever compensate for the energy wasted in doing it. *Or the misery.* Life is too short.

So is there a middle way that combines the ease of 'no dig' with the productivity of 'double dig'? *Of course!*

It's Yeoman's Lazy Sod.

The joy of Lazy Sod is you can make it any time in the year (though Autumn is ideal), on almost any weed-infested or rocky soil (provided it's not hopelessly polluted or acidic) and with a minimum of spadework. After it's made, you need never dig it again.

Yes, unlike other methods suggested here, you *do* need to wield the spade. But gently.

1.   Assume you start with a lawn, paddock or weedy plot. If the weeds are tall, slash or strim them back to ground level and leave them there. No other ground preparation is necessary.

2.   Mark out a rectangle of any convenient length and around six foot wide. This will give you ultimately a growing area four foot wide, narrow enough to reach easily into

the middle from the sides, plus two paths one foot wide on either side.

3. Down the middle of the bed lay as much kitchen waste as you can scrounge from restaurants, neighbours and pubs.

You'll rarely provide enough from your own kitchen - though you can lay it successively over several months, if you wish, covering each layer thinly with soil or other mulch to restrain the odour.

Lay only such degradeable vegetable waste as you'd normally put in a compost heap, avoiding meat, fish and poultry scraps which would attract cats and rats.

A six inch deep layer will do fine - and is about all that most of us city dwellers can accumulate.

4. Now use your spade to cut a two inch deep slit in the soil at the sides of that six foot wide rectangle. Slice under the sod or topsoil, peel it back like a flap and fold it over the sides and top of the kitchen waste layer.

To hold down the flap of turf and fill the gap in the middle of the bed, dig another two inches of soil out of the path areas and spread it over the top of the bed.

You now have a 'club sandwich'...

Hack off the weeds

Lay kitchen waste on top, then turves from the paths

Top the lot with soil from the paths

It's up to one foot in depth - of rotting top growth, kitchen waste, turf or top growth, followed by soil. That's a good start to any compost heap! However, it has little nitrogenous material so, unlike a compost heap, is unlikely to get very warm.

> You now also have sunken pathways that can optionally be filled in with gravel, wood bark, old carpet or even (temporarily) cardboard.

You could successfully stop there but, if you do, you're inviting a big problem: **weeds.**

So first water the bed lavishly - a full hour with a hose is not too much, if your water bill can stand it. Then lay a further layer of at least six or eight sheets of well-soaked newspaper over the bed, or a few sheets of cardboard, and hold them down with an inch of soil.

 Beware: lawn clippings are sometimes advised as a mulch. They work for a while, but then rot down to nothing - and meanwhile they harbour molluscs.

The turf sides will hold in the moisture and the newspaper or card will stop most perennial weeds fighting their way back, for at least a season. Any annual weeds that sprout from the top layer have little root structure and can be easily pulled.

> If nettles, dock, thistles, couch grass or other perennial weeds are a big problem, cover the newspaper with a further layer or two of thick

cardboard. Collect all the cardboard you need from the free boxes usually available at supermarket checkouts or, less formally, at their back doors.

You now have a tall *Club Sandwich*

At planting time, simply cut holes in the newspaper or card, dig out little pockets and fill them with sterilised top soil or compost. *And plant!*

For lettuces and small plants, you could drill half-inch holes in the cardboard using a cordless drill and insert spills of home-made seed tape (see **YOG qv**).

It's really fast and easy

I found a Lazy Sod bed around ten foot long can be made in two hours, excluding the watering, if all the materials are to hand. With one days' work - though I have never done this, disliking work - you can probably Lazy Sod an entire 40 foot allotment. (Try double digging it in that time!)

If you plan to grow moisture-lovers like cucumbers, beans, tomatoes, courgettes, pumpkins, marrows, potatoes, etc, you can make Lazy Sod just a few weeks before planting them. They devour even raw kitchen waste, provided you set the plants above it in several inches of topsoil.

For tubers, you'd be better advised to leave the bed for a year to rot down, and grow moisture-loving plants meanwhile.

Beans are especially useful as a first crop in Lazy Sod as their roots will add further nitrogen to the bed. Potatoes are also helpful in a new bed as grubbing them up later aerates the soil layers.

Lazy Sod is very versatile

Other ingredients can be layered in the bed according to the plants you want to grow.

For potassium-loving cucurbits, beans and tomatoes, add a double handful of wood ash every square yard (or square metre) to the soil layer just below the newspaper, and rake it lightly into the soil.

For heavy feeders like potatoes and beans you could mix raw farmyard manure in with the kitchen waste, but in temperate climes like the UK this must be done at least six months before planting - eg. in Autumn - to allow it to rot, heat up and cool down.

 Beware: be careful about adding lawn clippings to kitchen waste. Too much will turn your Lazy Sod into a steaming compost heap.

If you have plenty of leaves, mix them with the kitchen waste but in a ratio no more than one part leaves to two parts waste. They'll help aerate and drain the bed. (Too many have the opposite effect.)

Confine sawdust or wood chips, if you have them, to the top mulch layer. They decay only slowly and, unless mixed with ample rotted manure, will rob the bed of nitrogen.

At the end of the season, you should have magnificent plants, a much sunken but gently rounded raised bed plus the first major signs of weeds pushing through the now-rotted newspaper or card.

Pull out the plants (leaving the roots of beans in the soil, of course, so their nitrogenous nodules can fertilise the soil). Add another layer of kitchen waste and/or manure and/or spoiled hay or straw (if you can get it). Cover the bed with fresh newspaper/card, weight it down with a little topsoil and - you've protected the bed against weeds and erosion for the Winter.

Purists could protect the top instead with an over-wintering green manure crop then hoe it in at Springtime. But for me, that's too reminiscent of manual labour...

Lazy Sod is a low-maintenance strategy!

The odd sprinkling of bonemeal, lime, kelp or other organic correctives is fine, if the soil demands it, and a weekly feed of potassium-rich comfrey tea will doubtless help the beans and tomatoes. But there's no need to add chemical fertiliser, nor should you.

In early Spring, renew the now-rotted sheets of newspaper/card and start planting as before.

In this way, you can keep Lazy Sod going forever - without any further digging whatsoever.

Lazy Sod in a shower stall

To show the typical layers in Lazy Sod I made this example in an old shower stall flanked with carpet. I started with a thin layer of straw to simulate cutdown weed growth, added a thick layer of vegetable kitchen waste, then turf cut from the paddock and turned upside down, followed by rough topsoil.

No, I didn't cheat: I left in all the perennial weed roots.

I mixed in a good sprinkling of wood ash, soaked it all liberally and finished with a thick layer of wet newspaper followed by cardboard.

In that 12 inch sandwich I planted hungry feeders like courgettes and tomatoes. *And I never watered it*, rain apart, from that moment on.

Frankly, I've never seen such luxurious bombinaceous fruits.

Proof, as you see, that you can make Lazy Sod - and grow prolific plants - *anywhere!*

SUMMARY: THE 'INSTANT' NO DIG GARDEN

Here is one recommended way to turn a raw paddock or untended plot, infested with every kind of perennial weed, into a weed-free garden in 12 months. Without digging.

I offer it to anyone who has a 'worst case' garden. Its advice differs in small details from that given elsewhere.

Start in Winter, if possible. Strip off the top 2 inches of weed growth with a turf cutter and - where beds are to go - lay the turf back, upside down, to rot into compost. Remove the turf entirely from path areas and lay that on the beds too. Make these beds no more than 4 foot wide for easy access from the pathways and never walk on the beds.

According to the plants you intend to grow, spread extra compost on the beds, or rotted manure or - for heavy feeders like runner beans - even kitchen waste. Cover the entire paddock in thick green builders plastic (not the pricey black permeable stuff).

Swathe that plastic with a very thick mulch of wood chips, spoiled straw or the like. Come Spring, pull back the mulch, cut holes in the plastic and drop in transplants you've grown elsewhere. Fill gaps around the roots with sterile soil or compost. Push back the mulch.

This will grow most vegetables and flowers

This will grow most vegetables and flowers except carrots, parsnips and other roots which need well-drained friable soil. Potatoes can even be grown on top of the plastic. Cut a small hole in the plastic so the potatoes can root into the soil. Lay the chitted potato on the hole, then cover with mulch. Keep 'earthing up' with mulch as the leaves appear. When the foliage dies back, excavate the potatoes from the mulch. (This is the reverse of the well-known method for growing potatoes *beneath* plastic.)

After 12 months, other vegetables can be planted in the existing holes on a rotation basis. Or the plastic can be cut away entirely from selected beds.

The perennial weeds should be dead and the ground friable enough to rake. Now even carrots and parsnips can be planted in the open soil, using mulch between the rows to suppress annual weeds.

The only real problem with using thick mulch, as we've already seen, is that it harbours slugs and snails which can crop your transplants in one night. So cover every new plant with a mini-cloche - a plastic cola or milk bottle with its cap removed and base cut out - until the plants are developed enough to fight their own battles. (See elsewhere here for advice on mollusc invasions.)

This method does incur some front-end cost and labour (though far less than double digging). Getting mulch cheaply is easy in the country - put a classified ad in the local press and farmers will happily unload their rotten bales on you, often free.

Once done, little further maintenance is needed except to top up the mulch each year where the plastic remains. "You'll never see another perennial weed in your lifetime," my permacultural advisor assured me. *Hm...*

TEN ORIGINAL WAYS TO TAKE THE BACKACHE OUT OF GARDENING

Sweat, toil and gardening should never mix. That's *Yeoman's Second Rule of Lazy Gardening*. (The *First Rule* is: Let somebody *else* do the work you don't like.)

So here are ten ingenious strategies for those who dislike exercise, especially in the garden.

1. Make furrows in one tenth the time.

That artful gardener William Cobbett* described a simple rake that allowed one man to draw precisely straight drills for seed planting in a few moments. For carrots that were planted in 5 inch rows, you would take a sturdy lathe four foot in length and nail nine pointed wooden teeth along it, each at five inches from the other. The centre of the lathe was affixed to a broom handle.

Assuming that the ground was fairly moist but friable (if it isn't, you shouldn't be drilling seeds), you drew the rake along the plot to give nine furrows.

You then placed the rake's outermost right-hand tooth in the outermost left-hand furrow and repeated the exercise to draw eight more furrows. And so on.

Result: several perfectly 'drilled' rods of land - a rod is 14 feet - in less time than you'd need to savour a cup of tea. (Actually, Cobbett despised tea. *Sorry, I digress again...*)

It seems Cobbett kept several such rakes, with teeth set at different distances for different seeds.

Methinks, today's home handyman could easily make such a rake, but using a **metal** bar pre-drilled to take adjustable 'teeth' - such as large bolts - that could be screwed in and placed at any desired distance.

2. Block-plant seeds at exact intervals

Devotees of raised bed and French intensive gardening know that you get more plants if you abandon rows - and grow them in blocks. The ideal is to set them out equidistant on each side so that, when full grown, their leaves just meet on every side. This dense canopy suppresses weeds and conserves moisture, without starving the leaves of light.

 Tip: if you plant on a curved raised bed you get 150% more plants, as you can set them far closer together than usual without crowding their crowns when grown.

Problem is, planting in this way is a back-bending chore. So here are several ideas to minimise the ache:

3. Cut a cardboard hexagon.

This is a six sided template, made from card or thin wood. The distance between each of the six points should be your intended distance between the plants. Make a large hole in the middle and you'll find this too is the same distance from each point. Now you can position seven plants at equal distance from each other to make maximum use of the ground area.

With a long-handled dibber, press a hole in the soil at each of those seven points. Then flip the hexagon over on one side and make five further holes. Continue flipping the hexagon and pressing holes till the entire bed area is perforated.

Of course, you don't want to have to go back again and deepen those holes, so make them the right depth and width to receive your seed the first time. The easy way to do that is with...

4. A long-handled dibber

For large seeds like beans, onion and potato sets, sharpen the end of a broomstick - but ensure the 'sharp' end is gently rounded. Now you can press holes into moist soil of exactly the right depth and width, without bending.

A too-sharp dibber creates an air hole beneath the seed, which is not desirable.

To make deep and wide holes, eg. for seed potatoes or jerusalem artichokes, screw on a metal shelf support nine inches above the bottom of the dibber, to press down deeply with your foot.

For this, you'll need a dibber stronger than a broomstick, such as a 2in x 2in stake with a tapered rounded end. Screw *plus* lash that shelf support to the stake with strong wire or plasticated washing line. (Screws alone tear out in moments, I found.)

To plant the seeds, effortlessly, in these holes use...

5. A remote seed inseminator

This is a hollow pvc tube - cheaply obtained from plumbing suppliers. (I removed the downflow pipe from my greenhouse roof.) Just put it over the hole and drop in the seed! Many an onion set have I planted that way, most of them the right way up...

If you've already made **'seed tape' qv** you could plant even small seeds such as brassica, lettuce, carrots and parsnips in these holes very precisely. Cut the tape into squares, each containing some two seeds. Ball and moisten it (one's mouth does very well), and drop it down the tube. Then scatter fine sand or sterilised topsoil over the holes.

A Tip: if you do plan to ball up your seed tape, make it with absorbent **toilet paper** - not newspaper or kitchen paper. Then the germinating seeds have less work to do, to push through the paper layers.

If you prefer to cut conventional long furrows, eg. for peas, it's easier to use a tube curved at the bottom (like my greenhouse downflow) so you can drag it along the furrow, inserting seeds as you go.

Small seed can also be sown easily in furrows if you mix it with sugar or fine sand (lettuces), or polished rice or pearl barley (brassica and tubers). Cut a plastic milk carton or cola bottle in half, make a small hole in a bottom corner, and lash the carton to a cane.

Half fill it with the seed/sand mixture, hold the cane at the top and walk along the furrow, whistling merrily and dribbling out the seed as you go.

To set out plants rooting in loo rolls, or naked root balls such as those grown in Rootrainers or plugs, there's nothing for it but to get down to the soil and press them in to pre-made holes by hand. Even so, the task is simpler if you've previously made holes of exactly the right size, using a long-handled custom-made dibber.

> For example, the rectangular wedge-shape of a Rootrainer calls for a rectangular, softly pointed dibber, around 12 inches long and 1.5 inches square.

And here's a tip you'll find a mite eccentric, but it works...

6. For the backward gardener, a Butt-Pad

The real ache in gardening comes from constant bending, you'll probably agree. But bending _sideways_ from a seated position is less tiring. So why not replace your rubber knee-pad with...

a Butt-Pad?

Take a large foam plastic cushion, or a baby's changing mat. Sit on it, between the beds, and drop in your plants by leaning - _sideways._

If your holes have already been made, it's effortless.

Tomato plants - especially leggy seedlings - can be grown by simply laying them when they're 6-8 inches tall on the _top_ of friable soil, heaping earth over the rootball and their stems (all the way to the top leaves), and propping up the top leaves with a large rock or mound of soil.

No hole, no digging! Provided the soil was loose to start with, they'll develop a thick root system all along the stem, grow upright, and you can go back and stake them at your leisure.

> Yes, it _does_ work. (Just don't try it on heavy compacted clay.) I suspect it might serve equally well for beans, squash, courgettes or many other large well developed transplants.

Of course, it's well known that chitted potatoes can be grown by laying them on top of friable soil and covering them with straw or black plastic. When the plastic bulges, cut a slit to let the potato shoots poke out. Then grub under the plastic a few months later to harvest the new potatoes.

Again, no digging. And you can now plant potatoes with ease - from a recumbent posture.

That champion of No-Dig gardening, Ruth Stout, simply scattered *every* kind of seed over the naked earth - from onion sets to carrots. Then she laid, according to the size of seed, between 3 and 8 inches of straw over it.

> She sprinkled fine topsoil or sand over small seeds, of course, and kept the mulch off them. When the shoots had emerged, she drew the mulch up to them.

Her followers have gone even further. Noting that his most vigorous tomato plants were volunteeers ie. they'd somehow self-seeded, one lazy fellow just drops a ripe tomato here and there in Autumn, and covers it with straw. Next year, *lo*, a tomato plant!

You could do all this while sitting on your Butt-Pad.

Weeding also becomes pain-free this way and, if you use a changing mat, you can put the plants or pulled weeds on the mat between your legs and drag them with you. (Be careful with thistles, won't you?)

To move along the path, simply lift your butt and pull the mat. Backwards.

Scoff not. This idea is a boon to those like me who have back troubles. Why are Butt-Pads not sold at garden centres? (I suspect they will be, now this book has been published.)

Moreover, your upright-sitting posture lets you enjoy your garden from a wholly new angle, detect caterpillars and molluscs previously invisible under leaves, and smile at frogs and toads before - discovering you - they hop away.

And your hat no longer falls off.

If the excitement proves too much, you can sink back onto the path and annhilate all that's made to a green thought in a green shade...

Until your spouse turns on the sprinkler.

7. Watering in the rootball

Cobbett had a final tip for planting rootballs in holes made with a dibber, which would also apply to roots grown in loo rolls. (He had a full set of different-sized dibbers, of course. But he was sadly unacquainted with loo rolls.)

To firm the soil around the top of the plant is useless, he averred, if there's an air hole at the bottom. So sink the dibber alongside the plant, once planted, and pull the top of the dibber away from the plant. The end of the dibber will thus press into the bottom of the rootball, closing any air gaps.

Cobbett *didn't* say this but... it would make sense to leave the new hole open - then fill it copiously with water. This brings moisture to the base of the roots and closes the hole.

In fact, Cobbett was adamant one should *not* 'water in' newly set out plants. They wilt at first but - if the soil is already moist - they soon recover and grow stronger roots, he said, pointing out that extra watering inhibits early root growth.

As this advice contradicts most modern textbooks, it's almost certainly right. *Is it worth a test?*

8. Weeding without work

For organic gardeners, the only sensible long-term solution to weeds is to suppress them with mulch, as we've explored here many times. But often you need to clear a patch or hoe a row this season and it's no consolation to your painful spine to ponder what lovely compost those weeds will make - *next* year.

So.. lay cardboard or dark plastic over the lot, leave it for two weeks, pick it up and drop the lurking molluscs into heavily salted water.

> **A Tip:** later, you can prettily mulch a favourite indoor plant pot with the snail shells.

The remaining weeds will be dead - or soft enough to be hoed easily. Some gardeners recommend laying *clear* unperforated plastic in hot weather, so the sun fries the weeds.

Annual weeds are best cleared by hoeing the ground exactly ten days after you've cleared it, it's claimed. The new shoots, mostly invisible, die and your weed problems plummet.

This won't remove the deep-rooting perennials but tuberous weeds like dandelion, dock or nettles can be killed by cutting them at soil level then pouring salt thickly over the cut stems. (Yes, it's worth repeating, because it ruddily well *works*.) If you dig up the root yet accidentally break it, leaving the tip, pour salt into the hole - or it will grow again.

 Beware: use salt with precision, like a contact poison; too much of it will spoil the soil and kill earthworms, as Cobbett noted.

Paradoxically, he also recommended salt as a **fertiliser** - as much as "30 bushels" for an average garden. (Indeed, modern research suggests that 1oz of sea salt per sq yard *does* give increased yields.) In those joyful 19th century days, of course, an average "garden" for Britain's middle classes was many acres...

How to aerate your compost heap

To remove large weeds, you can buy a metal claw that - it's said - with a twist plucks out the offending beast. Alas, it works only in friable soil, leaves the deepest roots untouched and you could do a far better job on perennial weeds with a post hole digger (a long thin spade).

But such claws are fine... *in the compost heap*. Sink them deep, twist and pull. They mix the layers and bring in air, with less effort than tossing everything with a fork.

9. Stop bending - with raised beds

Disabled gardeners have long known the value of growing plants in beds 1 or even 2 foot high, so they can be tended from a wheelchair. There's wisdom in that for everyone, if you can suffer the initial labour or cost of building them.

In theory, they let you import exactly the soil you want, a perfectly balanced mix of humus - sterilised, of course, so perennial weeds won't be a problem. Your paths can be permanent: concrete, brick, gravel - even old carpets. An *Astrakhan* pavement?

But raised beds don't come cheap...

It's not the sidewalls that necessarily cost a Charlie's ransom. (They will, of course, if you buy in a truckload of old railway sleepers at £10 each and stack each at least three deep on all sides, well staked and secured - as you must, for a deep bed).

You can knock up walls by yourself for nothing, using old timber salvaged from a development site.

Or hire a jobbing handyman for £40 or so per day, who - wood scrap and electric saw in hand - should furnish out your entire allotment in little boxes for less than £100.

Your big investment is - **the soil.**

In the country, at least, you can get a big cartload of 'topsoil' for under £50. But it will contain every perennial weed root known to the Botanica. To buy in tons of *sterilised* topsoil, or compost, you'll need to win a lottery.

Solution? Well, you have to compromise.

Assuming you have your bed sides erected, just adapt the principle of **Yeoman's Lazy Sod qv!** The following strategy is, however, subtly different - as you'll doubtless note.

First, if you have any *totally* immortal perennial weeds like horsetail or couch grass, lay thick manure sack or silage bag plastic on the ground. It will suppress them long enough for your lifetime.

> They'll leap anew a century hence, of course, for your grandchildren to wrestle with. But meanwhile, that's Not Your Problem....

But if you're sure you're free of perennial weeds, just hoe off the top weeds and leave them there to rot.

Then spread a very thick layer of raw kitchen waste; a foot is not too deep, if your intended bed is two foot high.

Cultivate your local independent supermarkets and restaurants for vast binfuls of smelly throwaways.

Cover it thickly with straw, hay, rotted leaves, indeed any rottable fibrous waste. 'Spoiled' hay or straw is often available free from riding schools or farms. Pay them £5 or so for their petrol, and they'll often deliver it.

> **Beware:** you don't want too much manure or urine mixed in. By 'spoiled', I merely mean it's been out in the rain too long.

> Nor should you add lawn clippings. All that nitrogen would turn the bed into a fiery compost heap. Our object is to use it to grow plants - at once!

On top of the bed, lay enough compost to fill it to the rim, if you can get compost cheaply. If you can't, use sifted unsterilised topsoil and sand, mixed two parts soil with one part builders sand.

Sifting should get rid of most of the perennial weed roots (burn anything fibrous, especially if fat, succulent and white).

To sift large volumes, make a giant sieve use 1 cm or 1/4in wire netting, securely nailed over eg. an empty window frame.

This is not yet a perfect soil mix, by any means.

Passionate gardeners would mix into the top layer some form of slow-release organic nitrogen like blood, bone, fish and hoof meals - around a handful per square yard. *Or* wood ash, for potassium. *Or* peat, for moisture-retention and fibre. *Or* vermiculite, for drainage. (You'll need a second lottery win, to afford peat or vermiculite in such quantities).

They'd scatter dried seaweed and volcanic ash and, at the right phase of the moon, make voodoo passes...

But we're trying to make things sensible, not least on our wallets.

Finally, plant in those beds a vast quantity of heavy-feeding plants like tomatoes, beans, courgettes, pumpkins or other cucurbits. Even potatoes or comfrey. Make sure those beds are watered heavily.

To keep down the annual weeds, lay over the top thick blankets of cardboard, newspaper, carpet or other mulch (even old blankets). Whether you prettify that with a further sprinkling of compost, sawdust or wood bark is up to you.

 Grow more plants the first year than you think you'll ever need. Seed is cheap and you can always give away the spare produce or barter it for a brace of guinea pigs.

A Tip: guinea pigs are an investment. They'll devour your surplus carrots and deliver bushels of manure to kickstart the compost heap.

Your task, the first year, is simply to prepare the beds - and the excess plants will help you.

Result: those gross feeders will work their roots deeply into the bed and flourish, despite - and because of - the raw kitchen waste. Add several handfuls of earthworms at the start, if you wish, and those worms will pollulate - and ventilate your bed with their holes.

The beans will create extra nitrogen in their roots. So don't remove the roots from the beds when the plants are finished. And the heap will rot down to around one half its depth after one season.

Now you have a fruitful, fertile (half) raised bed that - I hope - has cost you very little. Build it up, and keep building it. If you're going to grow similar hungry-feeders next year, just repeat the process above.

If you *do* repeat the process, rotate the plants across different beds. True, some gardeners report they have successfully grown tomatoes and beans, without pest or disease buildup, in the same beds for decades. *But, if you have a choice, why risk it?*

However, comfrey is a perennial that should stay where it is, ideally dividing and re-planting the roots every 3 years or so. You can eat comfrey like spinach - or use it to make that wondrous fertiliser **Comfrey Tea qv.**

If you plan to grow tubers, omit the raw kitchen waste next year and mix in lots of sandy topsoil instead. If brassicas, mix in compost or well-rotted manure in Spring - or raw manure the Autumn before.

Oh dear, have I said all that, already - elsewhere? *Yes...*

If you didn't notice, you just weren't paying attention. But I make no apology. My few modest words in section 9 are - quite simply - the secret of stress-free joyful gardening. *Just do it - and see!*

That's nine tested good ways to make your gardening backache free. What's the tenth?

10. Declare your garden an urban-aerobic Ecocise gymnasium

Charge folk £10 an hour to dig, weed and mulch your garden - jogging round your plots to disco music while you lie in bed. And - lavishly using the words 'community', 'health', 'sustainable', and 'resources' - *get a Lottery grant for it.*

* *The English Gardener*, William Cobbett. Bloomsbury. 1829.

Seven totally lazy & novel ways to make good compost

Here's the ultimate compost test: is it so sweet-smelling and friable that you'd cheerfully use it for a mudpack - *on your face?*

Well, that may seem a little extreme but it wasn't so long ago that head gardeners tested for the best time to plant sweetcorn, by pressing their naked bottoms to the soil. It told them all they needed to know about soil temperature.

For all I know, mineral-rich compost might well make an excellent restorative face mask. *Another Yeoman breakthrough?*

Of course, there's a world of difference between creating good compost and a smelly half-digested mess that's fit only for the bottom of a bean trench. I discovered that in the early years, by making compost the *wrong* way.

Using four pallets bolted together to make a cube, I started in Spring with a layer of rough weeds and bracken, then grass clippings, then kitchen waste scavenged from my local pub, then the scrapings from the guinea pig cage. More household waste went on, then more grass clippings, till the bin was full.

It shrank in two months by two-thirds, so I started again, using the same ratios of 25% nitrogen (grass) to 75% carbon (household waste), just as the textbooks advised.

Alas, being as lazy then as now, I did not turn or mix the layers. Or protect them from rain.

In Autumn I shovelled out that disappointingly small amount of compost (five foot had dropped to little more than two foot). The top compost was reasonably friable and sweet but the deeper I dug, the more rancid it became. The last foot was a stinking wet green sludge.

> *Why?* I had not kept rain out of the heap so the compacted bottom grass layers, instead of composting, had fermented.

Hm... I had no wooden board to hand to lay on top of that heap, and any plastic sheeting would have blown away in the typhoons gusting from our Chiltern hills. But I *did* have masses of thick cardboard.

Thank heavens for cardboard

So next season, I began the heap in the same way, sandwiching grass clippings with kitchen waste. But this time I laid thick torn strips of cardboard over each mixture of grass/waste. The cardboard fragments let in some moisture but kept the deluge out.

As the heap rose, the cardboard on each layer rotted, contributing a little carbon of its own. I then stuck in *vertical* columns of cardboard, bent into square hollow tubes, pinched together and stapled at the bottom, and slashed with big holes every six inches at the sides.

That way, I could water the tubes periodically using a hose, so the compost got moisture at every level and was also well aerated.

> Some folks lay perforated PVC tube horizontally and criss-cross throughout the heap, to ensure ventilation.

> I think a better idea would be to insert a 3in wide perforated PVC tube in the shape of a U, with the bottom of the U lying across the base of the heap.

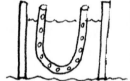

> As the compost heats up, it draws air into the heap. The tube also lets you add water.

Over the top, I laid a large sheet of cardboard to keep out the deluges yet hold in the damp.

By Autumn, I had a compost sandwich. The top cardboard layers were half-rotted between the good compost layers and could be easily removed to another heap. But the bottom layers - plus the cardboard ventilating columns - had turned entirely into good friable compost.

All of it sweet enough to rub on your face...

The Cardboard Sandwich approach is especially attractive because it avoids the chore of turning the heap every few weeks (who needs manual labour?).

Besides, some of us truly *do* have back problems. We're just not able to turn a ton of compost every fortnight or even, sometimes, lift a forkful of it.

Try a Sandwich - and your back (and garden) will bless you!

This year I also plan to try the idea, well documented by compost gurus, of supplementing my grass clippings (nitrogen) with balled up newspaper (carbon) in a 1:3 ratio. The balls let in air.

That should help those of us who, short of begging from local restaurants, never have enough carboniferous kitchen waste. But who *do* have vast piles of scrap newspaper to recycle.

Since I discovered The Joy of Composting, my life has gained a whole new fragrance...

Even cleverer compost ideas

Compost can be made very quickly using a tumbling composter. A big metal barrel with baffles inside to toss the compost about is mounted on a formidable structure of gears and ratchets so you can turn it regularly with a crank.

Frankly, I think anything which must be turned every day by a crank, probably is.

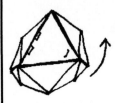 A cleverer idea might be to build a 12-sided wooden box like a geodesic dome, each side being a perforated triangle 18 inches wide. One triangle is hinged so you can open it to add material or remove the compost.

Being inherently unstable, it can easily be rolled around the garden like a giant beach ball, I suspect, even when full. Just push it over. This should build giant thighs and mighty biceps and make compost very quickly.

Conceivably, a large rubble sack - the indestructible kind that lifts several tons of sand - could be mounted within a contrivance of three interlocking metal hoops somewhat like a gyroscope.

You could then promote a team 'soccer' event, in which your neighbours compete to roll the Compost Ball into each others' goal.

A good evening's fun for all should yield you magnificent compost and bring new meaning to the phrase 'mucking in'. *Or am I, alas, getting carried away?*

SIX UNUSUAL WAYS TO TRANSPLANT & GROW ANY PLANT

especially parsnips, carrots, beetroot, turnips or skirret

Some time in the last millennium - in the Golden Age of Gardening, before the tv entertrainers coiled like noisome weeds around serious gardeners - there was a very silly Guru.

And he spake:

> 'Thou cans't not tranplant a parsnip. Nay, neither a carrot! Such will the act of transplant shiver and demoralise that fragile growth that all thereafter is just a waste of seed and a tinkling syllabub...'

He must have been a very powerful guru because today's textbooks still parrot: 'Thou can't transplant tubers'.

What compost!

Of course, you can transplant parsnips, carrots and almost anything else. Commercial growers have known that for decades, especially hydroponicists. How else could their businesses operate?

Here are seven ways to do it:

1. The Loo Roll Gambit

The simplest way is to plant in toilet rolls - whole ones for long tubers like carrots and parsnips (and for tomatoes or beans) and half ones for turnips and swedes, or indeed any small plant. (Moist compost will stay in place in the bottomless tube).

Put in a perforated seed tray in a plastic bag in a warm place till the seeds germinate and expect a powdery crust of orange mould to grow on the surface. It doesn't seem to harm the plants and vanishes

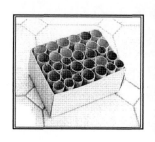

when you put the plants outside to harden off.

Beans growing in loo rolls

When the fronds are some three inches tall, insert the loo roll intact into a hole in the soil. The card will rot away and the tubers will continue to grow as if nothing had happened.

Beware: the card will take *several weeks* to rot away. So this is a tactic only for early crops or those with lots of growing time ahead.

2. The Newspaper Option

Newspaper rolls can be made in moments, in the absence of loo rolls, by wrapping some four to six sheets around a long 1.5in wide pole and taping with small tabs of sellotape at three inch intervals. Cut the tube into convenient lengths and plant as for loo rolls.

In fact, they're even better than loo rolls because they rot away faster. And it makes more sense than buying an expensive gadget to turn newspaper into pots!

3. The Origami Pot

Children enjoy creating novel paper plant pots, in nests of four. They're easier to fold using thin card - cereal cartons are ideal - but several sheets of newspaper also work.

Cut a square around 8in on each side. Fold each corner into the middle. Turn over and again fold each corner into the middle. Insert your fingers into the pockets created underneath and open them out as a little nest of pots.

Cut a small hole at the base of each pot.

These can be planted like half loo rolls and, when planting out, cut the pots apart and put them in the soil. By scaling up the size of your paper, you can grow pots of any necessary size.

> Okay, it's not a viable idea for serious growers - the pockets flop about in a vexatious manner - but it keeps the kiddies happy. Especially if you add a few pence to their pocket money for every tray they make!

4. The Naked Soil Block

Soil blocks are easily made without any pot at all.

Acquire a short length of 2in plumbing or gutter pipe. Cut a sturdy piece of wood into a circle that just fits the pipe, and screw on a handle to create a plunger - using a screw plus several washers or a bolt with a large head, so it protrudes.

A wine bottle of a suitable calibre does the job too.

You'll need to make your compost carefully so that it forms a block which retains its shape without support when watered.

Peat has traditionally been a major component of potless soil blocks but you might prefer to experiment with well-rotted and shredded leaf mould - or dried and flaked moss scraped off your roof - combined with commercial peatless seedling compost.

> *Or* buy several small packs of different seedling composts and see which retain their shape best in blocks.

Fill the tube around three inches deep with the slightly moist compost then compress it using the plunger. The protruding screw head leaves a shallow indentation, ideal for dropping in seeds then covering them lightly with loose compost.

The extruded blocks can be placed in a seed tray and, with careful handling, retain their form. The plant roots eventually grow out the sides where they are air-trimmed ie. they grow no further until transplanted.

I've no idea if this would work for tubers but am dubious, given the root handling that's inevitable when transplanting a naked soil block. However, it has worked very well for me for tomatoes, beans and brassica.

5. *The Egg Tray*

Okay, this is not a new idea but it works. Cardboard egg trays make useful starter pots.

A tip: put the empty half eggshells back in the trays and crack them a little around the bottom so the seedlings' roots can emerge. The shells also add a little calcium which - like continuous watering - helps avoid blossom end rot in tomatoes.

Cut them up when the seedling is tall and sink them in the soil, just like loo rolls.

6. *The Traffic Cone Secret*

Prize growers of giant carrots would never impart this secret to you because it's wickedly effective (and also illegal). But... if you should chance on a plastic traffic cone discarded in a tip, salvage it.

Bury it upside down in the soil, with the tip cut off to leave a two-inch wide hole for drainage and root development. Fill with a mix of sterilised sifted top soil, sand and a little well-rotted compost (but never manure).

Plant one tuber seed per cone, using seed from a 'giant' variety. In that protected hole, the tuber should wax enormous, even in otherwise poor ground.

> Of course, the cone belongs to your local council highways dept but, as it was discarded anyway, you might argue you were helpfully supporting the council's re-cycling dept... weren't you?

7. Rootrainers

I have had great success growing carrots (and almost everything else) with Rootrainers, a commercial product that consists of eight nests of four plastic seed pots, each just one inch square at the top but 8 inches deep - tapering like a long wedge. Each pot hinges open so the root ball can be extracted with minimum shock.

They save up to two-thirds of the compost you'd use for conventional pots, but give enough depth for tubers to establish firm root systems.

When my carrots had grown five inch fronds, I refrained from watering the pots for two days so the root ball was firm and dry. (Wet compost will just fall apart: the last thing you need when transplanting tubers.)

Then I rammed a nine-inch hole in the ground using a pointed wedge-shaped stake, and simply dropped in the root balls. (Or rather, root wedges.)

Beans and tomatoes can be grown in Rootrainers from seed to the point of planting out, without changing pots.

> I've never understood this nonsense of transplanting seedlings in several phases - from flats to successively sized containers - before planting out. Not only is it laborious but also it shocks the wretched plant a half-dozen times.

Rootrainers are costly but will last several seasons before becoming too brittle. (I'm into my fourth season, using them).

Good as they are, they're absolutely no substitute for loo or newspaper rolls, of course.

An idea you wish you hadn't read

When I was wrestling with some plastic plug trays, the costly flexible kind that is supposed to eject a tiny plug when you press it from below but doesn't, my plumber jested "You'd be better off using old condoms".

Well, why not? I'm told the SAS always carry condoms because they make excellent water containers and expand to unlikely dimensions. Consider how large a parsnip you might grow, in a condom!

For some reason or other, I have not tested this idea...

BETTER WAYS TO GROW SEEDS IN FLATS AND POTS - THE YEOMAN WAY

Germinating seeds is so simple. There really should be no problem in growing seeds in seedtrays or pots on your windowsill, should there?

I assume your daytime room temperature hovers healthily between 50o and 65o, ideal for all but the most exotic seeds. (Or those that need exotic treatment.)

So why do some fail to germinate or, worse, they get damping off disease - and rot before your eyes?

Maybe you've been heeding those wretched textbooks again.

Most textbooks tell you to plant your seeds in flats (seed trays), moisten the tray thoroughly by soaking it in a bowl of water and draining it. So far, so wise.

Then they tell you to cover it with a sheet of glass or perspex. On top, you put a layer of newspaper or whatever will exclude light. Every day, you take up the glass and wipe off the condensed moisture, and replace it, they say.

Even worse, they say, 'shroud each tray in a plastic bag'.

Frankly, I've never heard of a more foolproof way to guarantee damping-off disease...

Those seedlings will be either drowned, fermented, infected or poached to death - in the moisture that drips on them from the glass or plastic. Especially if you use a warm conservatory or greenhouse, or a costly electric incubator.

Besides, do you just happen to have lying around the house a few dozen sheets of glass or perspex - cut conveniently to the exact dimensions of your seed trays? More likely, as I once did, you'll slap on any old sheet of glass - then cut an artery when tripping over it.

Here's a better way.

Just cover those planted-out trays in... thick **cardboard.** Ensure a half-inch gap between the soil and cardboard. If cut more or less to size, the card will exclude light and also absorb the condensed moisture from the trays.

  Result: a humid atmosphere plus ventilation.

A slightly less efficient idea is simply to cover each seed tray with another seed tray stacked on top, so each gets a half-inch of ventilation but some humidity is still preserved.

Provided your trays or pots don't harbour disease to start with (scrub them with a mild bleach solution), both ideas *work.* I haven't had damping off disease since I used them. I've long been able to throw away my cans of Cheshunt solution. It had proved useless in protecting my seedlings from rot - *when I'd followed the textbooks.*

SIX FREE *LIQUID FERTILISERS*

Why buy fertiliser? Your garden or indeed almost any open heath or woodland can provide all the organic nutrients your plant needs, free.

Deep-rooting weeds like comfrey and nettles bring up trace minerals that may not even be present in some proprietary fertilisers, while having ample nitrogen, phosphate and potassium - the key N-P-K ingredients of bought-in plant foods.

A potent organic nutrient feed can be made simply by steeping comfrey leaves in a tub of water for up to three weeks, diluting that brown muck with five parts of water and pouring it on the plants. You can keep this pot going forever, by hooking out the decayed mass at the bottom for the compost heap then topping up with fresh weeds.

Beware: indoor gardeners please note - it smells *exactly* like fresh cow manure!

Comfrey is especially high in potassium, much needed by fruiting tomatoes, peppers, cucumbers, courgettes, melons, pumpkins and beans.

Your own witches' brew

For a more balanced nutrient solution, add nettles to that witches' brew. They are relatively low in potash but rich in nitrogen, which is important for leafy plants like lettuce and brassicas.

> Too much nitrogen makes leaves lush and languid, at the expense of fruit or flower formation, so moderation in everything...

Nettles can be infused by themselves to yield a potent feed, used occasionally, to boost pot and hanging plants that soon exhaust the nutrients in their compost. Dilute pure nettle tea ten times with water before use. And be advised, it smells even *worse* than comfrey tea.

There's no harm tossing into the comfrey-nettle tea a lesser proportion of yarrow, dandelion, chickweed or other common weeds. Each will complement the brew with its own trace nutrients.

If you grow plants with ring culture, or using any of the **Cola Bed qv** ideas, where the roots are wholly dependent on external liquid feeding, you can entirely substitute comfrey-nettle tea for proprietary solutions. Just be sure to feed daily. Or they'll grow yellow leaves, droop & be despondent...

Some gardeners suggest letting the weeds rot down by themselves in the tub without water. Comfrey will deliquesce all by itself into a thick murky liquor. This extra-strong brew should be diluted ten times with water before use. (Other weeds, I find, *must* have some water added while they're rotting down.)

This is a refinement?

A refinement is to put the weeds in a muslin or hessian bag before steeping them. (An old net curtain or pantyhose is perfect.) This filters out the muck, which is important to avoid clogging pipes and nozzles if you use the solution for hydroponics.

Hydroponicists who use wholly organic feeds recommend that the scrapings from a rusty nail be steeped in every four gallons or so of undiluted brew, to add iron which may not be adequately present in the weeds themselves. Some also sprinkle on a spoonful of powdered kelp (from health food stores), which is rich in trace elements.

Logically, lawn clippings should also yield a good nitrogenous liquid feed, if soaked like nettles, and provided they're free of weedkillers. (Grass juice is attested to be fabulously high in vitamins and minerals, which is why it's used in health cures.)

> **A Tip:** I've not tried this idea and can find no reference to it in my gardening library. *It merits experiment!*

Manure and compost teas

Similar nutrient feeds can be made using compost or manure, which are said to contain all trace elements. Put them in a bag before soaking or they'll disintegrate into slurry. Raw manure solution is very high in nitrogen and should be added with the same cautions you'd observe with raw manure itself. For example, keep it off tubers.

Wood ash and soot

A 'quick fix' liquid fertiliser can be made by soaking wood ash or soot, tied in a muslin bag in the same way. Ash and soot contain useful quantities of potassium and some phosphate and can also be added to nettle or manure tea, to complement their nitrogen.

Re-use the feed

Whenever practical, collect the liquid feed as it drips from the plant container and use it on other plants - for example, place the pot on two bricks over a tray, then collect the tray contents. A gallon or two of feed can thus supply an entire patio, if you're patient.

Domestic waste

The spent mash from home beermaking is rich in nutrients and can be soaked like manure, then strained and diluted.

The rinse or soak water from sprouted seeds, or water in which vegetables have cooked, is likewise useful: water the plants with it undiluted.

A fiercely nitrogenous fertiliser is human urine, diluted with five parts of water. Some organic gardeners add it in small proportions undiluted to comfrey-nettle tea, as well as sprinkling it on the compost heap - or on their heads.

Urine was recommended by the BBC during the last war as a dandruff cure.

Putting human urine on edible plants is controversial, of course, though urine is sterile and - once transmuted by the plant - quite safe.

Beware: human faeces, however, are totally *uns*afe to use in any form with edible plants, as are dog and cat faeces.

I confess that, having once watered my tomatoes for several weeks with the contents of the baby's potty, I was curiously reluctant to eat the tomatoes. However, permaculturalists have no such qualms.

I once had the privilege of stopping the night at the home of the editors of a leading magazine on sustainable living and found it difficult to locate their composting privy in the dark. So, I told them next morning, I'd been forced to open the bedroom window at 2am, shout *'gardez loo!'* - and fertilise the terrace pot plants.

I was joking. But they took me seriously. "We're honoured," they said. They assured me it was their custom too... *and I'm not sure they were joking...*

HOW TO GROW AN 'INSTANT' FOREST GARDEN...

and transform your backlot into Eden

Wouldn't it be nice if you had a garden ringed by food-producing trees, undersown with perennial vegetables and fruit - and, what's more, inter-cropped with shade tolerant annual veggies like cabbage, lettuce, squash and celtuce?

Suppose it would happily grow abundant food for your kitchen year after year, with little further care, fertiliser or weeding?

Yes, it's possible - if you grow a Forest Garden.

The idea was popularised by Patrick Whitefield in his excellent book *How To Make a Forest Garden* (Permanent Publications). He pointed out that tropical jungles have flourished for millennia, supporting food and wild life at every level from forest floor to treetop, without the intervention of man. Indeed, they've thrived all the better for man's absence.

Such a garden is indeed possible in the UK.

Once established, it needs almost no maintenance. The trees attract nesting birds, which add their little bit of fertliser to the soil. The trees also shade the plants below and drop leaves which mulch the ground, bringing further fertiliser while suppressing weeds and conserving moisture.

Edible berries like blackberries and raspberries plus perennial vegetables like 5-star broccoli, New Zealand spinach, land cress and the like will re-create themselves annually. Edible flowers like nasturtiums, calendula and tagetes will self-seed.

All you need do is wander those woodland pathways and sanctuaries, a glass of wine in hand, enjoying the wildlife and colourful change of seasons - and meditating.

But there's a snake in every paradise...

or three or four.

For example, you'll find only a handful of such gardens in the UK to date, and few have been established long enough to prove they work. That's not surprising as it takes many years to grow trees.

> Moreover, pictures I've seen of them look grim - a viscous mess of leaf mulch and tangled undergrowth. Can't a recreational garden also look, hm, *attractive?*

Plant big trees in a small urban garden and you may face interesting battles up the road from neighbours and planning officers.

For most of us with small urban plots - and inevitably a short time horizon before we sell up and move - to create a permanent 'tropical' jungle is just not realistic.

So... is it possible to create an **'instant'** forest garden that yields, albeit temporarily, all the benefits above - and more - *but in just one season?*

Yes! Welcome to Yeoman's Eco-Jungle.

Please forgive that trendy 'eco' prefix. It signifies merely that your garden will now actually give back to you more than you put in, year after year. With minimal work. And yes, it truly *can* be self-sustaining.

You don't need specially cultivated or rotivated soil. I grew my prototype jungle in a mature paddock, boasting just six or eight inches of hard clay above flint and chalk and infested with perennial weeds like couch, dock, nettles and thistles.

> As you've read before, it was also a resort hotel for snails and slugs.

You don't need to work too hard. Your only real labour comes in the first year and if, like me, you contract it all out to the local jobbing gardener you'll labour not at all - and spend less anyway than you might have done on a few packets of herbal cigarettes.

Next year, your costs and labour will drop to negligible levels. (Well, the labour is now fun - and that's not labour, is it?)

You won't need to wait more than five months to see good results. And you can repeat those results, year after year, indefinitely.

What's more, your 'instant' forest garden will - all by itself - deep-dig, improve and add nitrogen to the soil.

It will yield carbon-rich mulch, either for your compost heap or directly to the soil. It provides a plethora of strong tall canes to support next year's beans or sweet peas or other climbing plants, or to make rustic grow boxes, or to provide wood chips to mulch your paths or 'conventional' garden.

It attracts and feeds pest-eating birds. It suppresses weeds. It grows runner or climbing french beans in profusion. It provides umpteen kilos of edible seeds, for toasting as snacks, grinding into flour or germinating into lush sprouted greens - giving you fresh-food vitamins even in the depths of winter.

It shades your inter-crops of cabbage, lettuce and other brassica, and aromatic herbs, even alpine strawberries.

It quickly creates a a 12ft high (or more) canopy of beautiful bird and butterfly-filled jungle - with winding

paths and secluded spots wherein your children can play safely and you can disappear completely, to ponder the absurdities of life.

And no, unlike certain television people, we *don't* build it overnight with trellis, water features, decking and purple paint!

Oh how, great compost maven, might we gain this fabled haven? (I hear you ask.)

Simple. Imagine a jungle of giant sunflowers, which support climbing french or runner beans. Each of these 'food turrets' is inter-cropped with salads, brassica, or annual edible flowers.

Over the soil is a blanket of cheap green horticultural plastic (not the costly black 'permeable' kind which, I find, is anything *but* permeable). It's slitted to let in rain and has holes cut for the plants. And overlaying the plastic is a mulch of, well, anything pleasing to your eye -

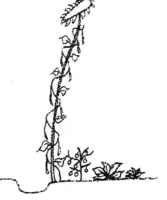

straw, dry leaves, sawdust, wood chips, bark, even sea shells, sharp sand, snail shells or pea gravel.

You don't need a paddock-sized area.

You can make a mini eco-jungle in a patch just four foot by six. This will grow around 16 runner or climbing french beans around the perimeter and as many as 24 seed-yielding giant sunflowers in all. *Plus* - around the edges - some 16 calendulas or tagetes, nasturtiums, herbs, small lettuces, mizuna or other salad plants.

You just won't have as much room to create a meditation sanctuary in the middle... Though I bet your children will dig one out, anyway.

Of course, these projections are theoretical. (That means I can nimbly escape from justifying them in every particular.)

For example, I'm making a lot of assumptions about your soil quality, available light, rainfall, wind exposure and local pests. If you're lucky, peacocks may visit your eco-jungle, beneficially (they'll eat the bugs), but so - certainly - will slugs, cats, rabbits and dogs - less beneficially. Yet we do have one or two remedies for four-legged, or no-legged, pests... *see elsewhere.*

> **Meanwhile, take note:** lion/tiger dung or urine from your local zoo dispels ALL four-legged pests fast, plus children, spouses and relatives. But put it above ground in a container like a perforated plastic milk carton, so it won't get into the soil.

Idle theory? Not at all.

Remember, not for nothing am I called the **Lazy Sod Gardener**. If any task spells 'work', I put my head back under the pillow.

So how do we set about transforming a 'so so' patch of ravished urban soil into a lush food-producing jungle?

First, start in Autumn or early Spring and get lavish amounts of compost into that soil. Or any organic matter will do. Lay...

> kitchen waste, hay, straw, scrapings from the guinea pig cage, leaves, grass clippings, cigar butts, shredded newspaper or cardboard, rotted farm manure (you can lay steaming fresh manure in Autumn and it will cool down by Spring), elephant and rhino droppings if you have them (and have you really, truly exploited the fertile potential of your local zoo?), even torn-up cotton or woollen clothing or blankets (but avoid synthetic fabrics).

Your old jeans, socks and underwear are fine, provided they're all cotton. And well shredded.

Beware: _don't_ lay cat or dog faeces, as I've said.

And avoid meat or fish scraps, at least in towns - they attract rats and cats. But in the country, where rodents abound anyway, just lay that offal a long way from the house. And cover it with soil to abate the stench.

In other words, enrich your soil now - because later it won't be as easy.

In Autumn or earlier, lay stuff that takes a long time to rot and in early-Spring (eg. February), put down quicker-rotting vegetable matter. Fork it in gently. Then walk away. The earthworms will drag it down without your help

I don't care if your sub-soil is a chaos of builder's rubble or a mattress of couch grass roots.

Provided you lay enough organic matter at the outset (a foot or more is not too much, if your soil is truly awful) and your soil has at least some earthworms in it, this method will give you some results.

But of course, the better your soil is in the first place, the better your results.

Second, around March or early April (in the UK), rotivate that land. You can hire a rotivator for a few pounds or borrow your neighbour's Mantis hand cultivator, which is fun to use but won't dig as deep. Or for a few pounds more, a jolly jobbing gardener will do it for you. It's a good investment, because you'll never have to rotivate that land again.

Your task is simply to mix up all that organic matter, well rotted or not, into the soil and make it friable enough for planting.

Question 1: Won't rotivating simply chop up the perennial weed roots and proliferate them?

Answer: Yes, it will. But you can forget about perennial weeds. The next step kills or suppresses them permanently (and without chemicals).

Question2: *Doesn't rotivation sometimes create a hard pan around six inches below the surface, which impedes drainage? Shouldn't I rather dig that soil, even double dig it, to get rid of the stones and break up the hard pan?*

Answer: if you want to be a masochist, double dig by all means. It does no harm and I'm told it's good exercise (I don't know: I've never done any exercise). But you're in the wrong book. This is not French Intensive or Biodynamic Gardening, admirable though they may be. It's Yeoman's *Lazy Sod* Gardening - with yet another delightful twist.

Stones are no problem by this method, within reason, and the next steps break up all but the hardest of hardpan, mostly by themselves.

Back to the Forest Garden...

Now water that plot. I don't mean, a few minutes with a watering can. I mean drench it for one hour, using a hose pipe. (If it has just rained copiously for 24 hours, and I do mean copiously, you may omit this step.)

Lay vast canopies of green builders plastic over the soil and hold it down with bricks, soil-filled plastic bags or planks.

A tip from experience: don't be tempted to economise by mulching with little squares of cardboard, newspaper or folded out plastic manure bags. Excellent though they are for *tactical* mulching, we're talking **serious long-term strategy** here.

Even if you overlap them, some perennial weeds will creep through the gaps and, for this method to work over the long term, you'll still have to replace them with continuous plastic eventually.

You can now leave the soil alone for a month or two for the organic content to rot down a bit more. If much of it remains unrotten come planting time, never mind. The crops you're going to grow there, sunflowers and beans, love water-retentive muck - even old woollen night caps - rotten or not.

Third, in early April (in the UK), start germinating giant sunflower seeds. Germinate them in your conservatory, greenhouse or on your window sill, following the packet instructions and using small three-inch pots.

Yogurt pots perforated at the bottom work well. Even better are loo rolls because, when the sunflowers are about five inches high, you can drop them - loo roll and all - straight into a bigger pot then, when 10 inches grown, into the soil with little root shock.

By the time the loo rolls rot, a month or so hence, the sunflowers will be strident.

Allow enough plants to cover your allocated plot at spacings of 1ft on all sides, and plant a few more too, to allow for non-germinating seeds.

Yes, this spacing is closer than your packet suggests, especially for giant sunflowers. But 1ft spacing will not deter a healthy sunflower, given adequate light, warmth and water. It also ensures the suppression of most weeds.

Fourth, in early June (in the UK), when the sunflowers are about a foot tall, plant climbing french or runner (snap) bean seeds in similar pots. Indoors on your windowsill or in your conservatory or greenhouse.

> Personally, I've found my conservatory far better for growing seedlings than my unheated greenhouse. In Spring, the termperature in the latter can richochet between -4oC and 40oC within 24 hours: fatal to seedlings. But my conservatory always stays within a tolerable 10oC-30oC range.

Plot your Forest Garden

Plant only enough beans as you'll have sunflowers on the outside of your plot.

So if you have only a small six foot by four foot eco-jungle, in theory you could grow 6 rows by 4 rows of sunflowers at 1ft spacing ie. 24. The sunflowers in the inner rows will seek their own light.

> Once well started, sunflowers will grow *anywhere* after a fashion, just like Jerusalem Artichokes, given light or

not. But your beans will grow *only* on the perimeter: in the early days, at least, they need full access to light. (Later, they admirably tolerate shade.)

That means, using the perimeter sunflowers as their support, you can grow 16 bean plants. Do a similar calculation for the plot you plan, whatever its size.

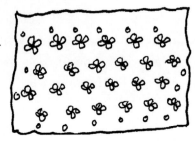

Of course, you could always plant *two* beans up each sunflower and as much as double your yield...

The point of waiting at least a month between planting the sunflowers and planting your beans is that the former need to become very well-established before they'll support the latter. But once you've seen an 18 foot giant sunflower - and despaired of breaking the 3-inch thick woody stem at its base - you'll have no doubt of its ability to support any bean, given a head start.

Two giant sunflowers together, I suspect, would support a fireman's ladder...

Fifth, in late May or early June (in the UK) any danger of frost should be past. So harden off your sunflowers and beans for a few days in a cold frame. Or put them outside by day and take them in at night.

I just transfer them to my unheated greenhouse for four days with all the ventilation slots open. I haven't the patience for all this daily 'bring them in, then take them out' hardening-off nonsense...

Then, using a sharp knife, cut four inch slits promiscuously all over the plastic on your slot, to let in future rains. And cut cross slits to receive your plants ie. make one six-inch slot and another one across it at right angles, fold back the plastic and tuck it underneath so you have a square five inches on each side.

Dig a hole one inch bigger and deeper all round than your transplant. Drop in the transplant.

 Great idea! If you've wisely let your sunflower shoots get well established first, you risk disturbing the sunflower roots when putting in the beans later.

Solution: when first planting out the sunflowers, sink a tin can beside them. A month later, you take the can out, drop in your bean rootballs, and the sunflowers won't even notice.

This tip will work if you plan to set *any* transplant close to an already growing plant, at a later date.

Fill the gaps with compost. Water copiously. (Using a solution of kelp or seaweed extract at room temperature at planting time is said to minimise transplant shock). Fold the plastic back around the stem, using small rocks to hold it down if necessary.

Or you could fill the holes with little pads of thick wet newspaper. That's also a great tip when planting brassica in plastic, as it totally defeats cabbage fly.

Plant the sunflowers at 1 ft spacing in both directions, then do the same with the beans, planting them only on the perimeter of the patch and four inches from and to the side of their adjacent sunflower.

Sixth, you have just two more tasks!

If you want your Forest Garden to be beautiful - downward as well as upward-looking - scatter a thick (2 inch minimum) layer of decorative mulch. Rotted leaves or spoiled straw are free but, in my garden at least, they provide a haven for snails ands slugs. So I used wood chip which seems less attractive to them. But almost any attractive biodegradeable substance will do.

And if you want your garden to be *super*-productive, consider - what gaps remain around the perimeter that you could fill with small edible plants or flowers?

Pot marigolds (calendula) or African marigolds (tagetes) are ideal, as are nasturtiums - you can eat both leaves and flowers, and the seeds pickled in vinegar. They attract beneficial insects and are workhorses for deterring pests.

Dwarf tomatoes and/or dwarf french beans are a natural.

How about small cos lettuces or mixed saladini (lolla rossa lettuce, radichio, chervil and the like) - which you can 'cut and come again'?

I think lazy gardeners should forget about chicory and endive. I find they taste disgusting, unless you go to great lengths to blanch them. And even then...

Land or American cress tastes just like water cress and grows year round, almost perpetually, even in shade.

These plants are indestructible?

Celtuce, corn salad, purslane, miners lettuce and the common but delicious 'weeds' - chickweed, dandelion and fat hen (lambs quarters) - are almost indestructible plants that either self-seed or can be nursed through the winter under a layer of straw or mulch.

 A Tip: These plants *never* in my experience give you significant pest problems. And I find them tastier than any conventional lettuce.

You'll need to seek out these exotic seeds from specialist growers or salvage them from weeds already in your garden.

Why not try the perennial or biennial herbs like parsley, thyme, oregano, marjoram or chives?

The more aromatic plants you grow as edging for the plot, the fewer problems you should have with pests.

The beauty of this method - literally so - is that, while your sunflowers and beans will be removed at the season's end, there's no reason why the perennials can't remain there indefinitely to protect and enhance next year's crop.

Okay, talking of pests, there's always a snake or two in paradise.

'No dig' gardeners have long discovered that thick mulch is a mecca for snails and slugs. Indeed, when I first used a 'no dig' bed I had a 'no vegetable' garden. But the molluscs paid little attention to my other transplants that were already five inches or more grown.

So provided your transplants have been well developed elsewhere, you should have minimal problems.

What else do you do? Nothing!

Provided your plot was well soaked before you laid the plastic, your transplants should grow sturdily all by themselves and gain enough supplementary moisture through the slits you made in the plastic, and from the half-digested organic matter you rotivated in.

A Tip: I once didn't understand that the point of digging a trench for beans in the Autumn and throwing in vast quantities of raw kitchen waste is not to fertilise the soil. It's to build a water reservoir! Beans need copious water, especially when forming beans, and that's more important than fertiliser.

I tested this. I planted one row of climbing french beans in my kitchen garden (not my paddock) in a trench strewn with kitchen waste to retain moisture. I planted an identical row in a trench merely sprinkled with potash-rich wood ash (fertiliser).

The 'kitchen waste' row yielded more than double the crop of the fertilised row. *Water is clearly the key ingredient.*

Or is it? I have just read a gardening guru who said that beans hate wood ash. So what's the true answer? *Oi veh...*

Of course, if there's a drought - water your patch. Once you get serious with a Forest Garden, you might want to lay leaky plastic pipes over the plastic sheet and under the mulch so you can trickle-feed water in dry weather.

> **Beware**: don't put them *under* the sheet, of course, as some textbooks advise. However will you get to them in future, to move or repair them?

This is the most efficient - and least-labour - way to water that I know. The slow seepage ensures maximum soaking, the mulch impedes evaporation and those ugly pipes are invisible and should never again need to be disturbed, except for occasional repair.

What have you achieved?

By early Autumn, you will have gained:

• *A beautiful stand of giant sunflowers.*

They will be the talk of your neighbourhood, especially if - like mine often do - some exceed 18 feet.

• You have attracted beneficial insects and birds galore, which devour the seed heads.

Be sure to shroud a few choice heads with fleece or pantihose before the birds get them all, then cut them to dry in a warm place. They're very decorative, hung in your conservatory or kitchen or over the hearth.

If you plan to re-plant the seeds next season, or sprout them to eat as succulent vitamin-rich greens all Winter through, remove them from the seed head immediately it's cut eg. by rubbing against a wide meshed sieve.

Lay them on kitchen paper at room temperature for a few weeks. When the seeds are dry, store them in a paper - not plastic - bag in a cool place eg. a fridge. The sunflower heads you hang in the kitchen for months may be pretty but... parched seeds just don't germinate.

• *You have a wagon-load of woody sunflower stems...*

some up to three inches thick. Dry and keep them under cover and they'll give you sturdy tripods next year to grow even more beans, or other climbing plants. Or shred them for compost or mulch.

Cut into one foot lengths and braided together with plasticated string or sash cord, they can be unrolled wherever needed to make decorative and surprisingly sturdy temporary pathways. (Now *there's* an idea!).

> *Or* they can be bound into cylinders as rustic growing pots.

Wind them into Gro-Spirals to grow healthful herbs. Cut into shorter lengths, they yield attractive edging for lawns and beds, at least for a season. Or chop and burn them in your grate - their calorific value approaches that of wood.

• *Plus, you've gained a 'natural rotivator'!*

Those sunflower roots will have penetrated as much as 20 foot into your subsoil, aerating the ground. That's why they can improve poor soil and even break up hard pan. All by themselves.

• *And what about all that fresh organic food?*

I nearly forgot the beans you grew... I hope you enjoyed eating them. You probably had enough to freeze, salt away and pickle too. But when it's time to cut them down, leave their roots in the ground. They contain nitrogenous nodules that add fertility for next season's crops.

Meanwhile, those fresh edible plants on the plot's perimeter should have kept your kitchen busy.

• *You have a haven on earth.*

If you've grown a Forest Garden that's big enough to stroll through, you've also enjoyed the walkways and quiet 'jungle' nooks among the sunflowers.

As the seedheads form overhead, they can easily persuade you that you're walking through a rainforest. Except that your *deep* enriched soil, curiously enough, is now far *more* fertile than the acid, sterile, thin bed of a true rainforest.

What do we do next year?

Keep planting out those sunflowers and beans!

Okay, I know we should really rotate the plot each year to minimise the risk of plant-specific infections building in the soil. But many allotment holders have been growing beans successfully for decades in the same plot. They have no choice: their 'bean tent' is a permanent steel and concrete fixture...

The No-Dig guru Ruth Stout has been growing tomatoes in the very same plot, successfully, for 20 years. She avers that, adding an 8-

inch mulch of spoiled straw every year buffers, renews and enriches the soil so pest buildup or soil deficiencies never occur.

If you're really concerned about crop rotation (or you have evidence of a crop-specific disease or pest in that soil), you could always replace - for two or three seasons - the beans with tomatoes, or squash, or cucumbers. Or any other climbing veggie or flower.

That said, next year you'd be wise to cut away the plastic from each bed and work in some fresh compost or organic matter. By then, some perennial weeds at least should be dead and the earthworms have turned your 'impossible' soil into a friable fertile bed, at least the top few inches of it.

If some perennial weeds come back - and mare's tail and couch grass roots seem to persist forever - put back the plastic.

After three years (make it a century, in the case of couch grass), your plot should indeed be weed-free and transformed.

You can then revert to conventional or raised bed gardening, happy that your deeply-worked soil will now support it.

Deeply worked, did I say? I didn't see us doing much work there, did you?

So what's wrong with mare's tail or Japanese knotgrass?

Personally, I think mares tail makes a *beautiful* edging plant - architectural, vigorous, big and fast growing (high in silica and good for scouring pots) and strikingly evocative of the dinosaur age, wherefrom it hails. I would cultivate it just for that purpose. Only fashion leads us to disdain it in our gardens.

A Tip: grow it from roots, contain its unwelcome vigour in a pot and **put it in your conservatory**. It's far more reliable - and arguably more gorgeous - than a parlour palm.

Equally, if I could get it, I would lavishly *plant* Japanese Knotgrass (that bane of gardeners) just for its delicious proliferating young shoots, much more luscious than asparagus - especially eaten with Hollandaise Sauce. (Of course, I would contain its growth in a cement trough.) If you have Japanese Knotgrass in your garden, may I please... *beg a root?*

Sunflowers and allelopathy

Some gardening writers have suggested that sunflower roots can be allelopathic to other plants - that is, they secrete toxins which suppress their growth. However, these suggestions may be merely anecdotal.

My own enquiries to the superb HDRA, the ultimate source of organic gardening experience, elicited the response in effect "we don't know". And they kindly referred me to the writers below. So I tested it.

Yes, growing sunflowers with beans works! I have the proof in my garden. The anecdotes are wrong.

But I will add one caveat. Both sunflowers and beans are very thirsty plants. Sunflowers may have gained their bad reputation as plant suppressants simply because - as Bob Flowerdew points out - they suck moisture away from other plants. You must keep your Forest Garden supplied lavishly and continually with water. Then both plants are happy. And so are you.

References to sunflowers and allelopathy:

Designing and Maintaining Your Edible Landscape Naturally, R Kourik.
The Complete Manual of Organic Gardening, B Koplan
The Complete Book of Companion Planting, B Flowerdew

THE ART OF (VERY) LAZY SPROUTING

How to Gain More Life-Energy with Less Labour

What does a lazy gardener do in the long winter evenings?

Sprout, of course. I'd just mulched my problem paddock in cardboard and black plastic, held down with soil-filled plastic bags to resist our gale force winds.

Having thus totally guaranteed my organic veggy supply *(ho!)* for the rest of the year, I wondered what to do with the rest of my day.

Create a garden in my airing cupboard?

And why not. Sprouts are notoriously nutritious. Just 1lb of fresh soybean greens has more vitamin C than a basket of lemons, more protein by dry weight than fillet steak and enough chlorophyll, it's claimed, to enable you to throw away your medicine cabinet.

That potent life-energy is cheap too: 1lb of fresh pea sprouts costs less than 8 pence if you buy your organic dried peas in bulk. But the sproutarian textbooks I bought with youthful enthusiasm some 25 years ago were written by raw-food pedants.

First, they made sprouting sound as threatening as agricommerce. Who has the time to study - in finicky detail - the food values, soak periods, rinse frequencies, growing times and temperatures for every edible seed on the planet?

Second, sproutarians are cradle-snatchers. They devour their sprouts raw and young, when the root has barely appeared. Yet the maximum flavour, and usually nutrition, is gained when the shoots are tall and in leaf. I also prefer those sprouts steamed or stir-fried. (Indeed, most bean sprouts - especially kidney - are toxic if not cooked.)

To my polluted palate, most recipes made with uncooked infant sprouts taste disgusting. There seems little point in trying to convert even willing disciples like me to a healthier food-style, if we can't eat the food...

So I soaked those books for 24 hours and sprouted alfalfa on them.

Here instead are...

Yeoman's Tested Rules of Lazy Sprouting (for non-sproutarians):

1. Forget methods that need hand-rinsing

All sprouts start the same way. Big or small, soak the seeds overnight. You can drink the soak water from wheat or barley grains. Called Rejuvelac, it's said to have fabulous nutritional properties and, despite that, tastes quite nice.

But other soak waters are too bitter or flatulence-forming or (in the case of kidney beans) too toxic to drink. Water the house plants with them.

At this point, however, my ideas diverge from the textbooks...

It's fun - the first time - to watch a tablespoonful of alfalfa or mustard seed expand to fill a quart jar in five days. But the jar, typically sealed with a nylon stocking and rubber band, must be laboriously rinsed at least twice a day. The sprouts are a tangled mess, nor do most grow fully or develop health-giving chlorophyll.

If you eat a lot of sprouts and/or have a family to feed, you'll need to start a new jar every day. Better make that three jars daily, if you also juice and drink your sprouts for optimum nutrition.

After a week your arm aches like a bellringer's...

Some large sprouts like sunflower, corn, soy and peas are best grown in seed trays on damp kitchen paper or a thin layer of moist compost. So - after two or three days inside a plastic bag to aid germination - the trays will need spraying twice a day. That's manual labour *(ouch!)*.

A lazier idea is to sprout all your seeds or pulses whatever their size, using a garden seed tray, all at once ie. with seeds of the same size put in the same tray, but with several trays stacked on top of each other.

Stack the seed-filled trays - the kind with drainage holes - on top of each other so in the early days they seal in humidity. When the shoots form, place between each tray another seed tray. This tray's empty, with its bottom cut out to allow the sprouts to grow upwards. It's positioned at right angles to the one below to hold the stack secure and let in light.

Then twice a day you merely water the top tray, using a watering can with a fine rose, and enjoy the musical drips as they percolate to the bottom. (Put a solid tray there, of course.)

Start a new tray every day and slip it under your pagoda. Harvest the top tray after five to 14 days, depending on whether you've sprouted alfalfa or wheat grass.

Result: a continuous supply of all the fresh salad greens one person should ever need.

2. Build a semi-automatic high-volume sprouter - in 20 minutes

Lazy sprouters like me balk at twice-a-day watering (or any manual watering). So an easier way is to buy eight rectangular plastic washing-up bowls (cheap at market stalls), 14 wooden lathes some one-inch square and 15in long, and a strip of capillary matting about five foot by 6in (clean blanket will do instead).

Perforate the bases of six bowls lavishly with a hot skewer or drill. Lay in each your damp kitchen towel, folded twice - but drape the rest of that towel over the top of the bowl and let it hang an inch down the back.

Then lay your pre-soaked seed as usual.

Stack the seed-filled bowls, separated by the wooden lathes, above an unperforated bowl and put the other unperforated bowl on top of the stack. Drape the capillary matting down the back of the stack so its top rests in the top solid bowl and its end is in the bottom solid bowl.

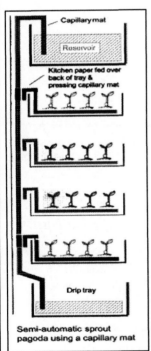

Capillary mat

Reservoir

Kitchen paper fed over back of tray & pressing capillary mat

Drip tray

Semi-automatic sprout pagoda using a capillary mat

Now fill the top bowl with water, to a prudent level. Important: make sure the 'wick' of damp kitchen paper rising from each bowl presses firmly against the capillary mat behind it, so moisture is transferred from the matting to the wick.

Eg: push the pagoda against a wall, and protect the wall from moisture with a plastic sheet.

Each tray should stay moist and need no further attention for up to a week, from just one filling of the top reservoir. (Make the flow to each tray stronger or weaker by trimming the width of the matting.) *Just don't trip over it...*

Go on holiday for five days and you'll return to six big bowls of fresh sprouts!

You could keep them fresh in the fridge for up to a week, cellophane-wrapped: the vitamin content of some sprouts actually increases under refrigeration. But, of course, you'd be wiser to build your pagoda gradually, adding a new bowl every day.

This method is simplicity itself and works with most seeds and pulses, if the room temperature stays between 60oF and 75oF. But... they will grow more slowly than by other methods because they're not rinsed or ventilated.

> **Beware:** That's why a hot and stagnant airing cupboard is, in truth, a *terrible* place for sprouts.

3. Yeoman's Lifetime Lazy Sprouting Machine - built in two hours

When you become serious about sprouts, you'll want to have a lot of them continuously to hand - yet do negligible work. Here's how - for just £45 - I built a simple machine in two hours that has reliably yielded me 8 sq ft of perfect sprouts every week, totally automatically, needs almost no maintenance and should last a lifetime.

It also jollies me with water music every twelve hours.

It's merely an open-fronted nest of shelves built to take eight standard perforated seed trays, each covered with kitchen paper. Each paper sheet is perforated a few times, to ensure good drainage. At base is a water cystern containing a submersible electrically-operated pump. This connects to a plastic hose which snakes to the top tray and ends with a fine-rose spray.

The pump is fitted with an electric timer that turns it on for 15 minutes every 12 hours. Water sprays from the rose, drips through the trays and collects in the bottom reservoir. It needs replacing only every few days (the rinse water is now a potent organic fertiliser).

Result: each seed is regularly watered (important for big seeds like peas and beans), and rinsed (mould from healthy seed rarely happens), and ventilated. Seeds grow up to twice as fast as when using capillary or manual watering.

That constantly agitated water should appeal to Feng Shui enthusiasts: it releases lots of healthy ch'i! My conservatory is much nicer to work in now I have a water feature that humidifies it, sounds delightful and is actually useful.

Cost? The only significant items were the water pump (£35), timer (£5), and the plastic hose and spray head (£5). For the wood, I traded some tomatoes with my plumber. He then found the cystern for me gratis from a building site.

Tip: Obtain a cheap low-power pump that will lift water little more than 4ft eg. Laguna PowerJet 500. You want it to flow, not spurt

You can use this system to germinate seed.

Stack the bottom two shelves with self-stacking trays two-up, so the double trays hold in the humidity. Immediately the seeds sprout, move each tray higher up the pagoda so it has ventilation and growing space.

For faster sprouting of hot-climate pulses like soy, sesame, kidney beans, sweetcorn, mung and other exotica which prefer 70oF-80oF, shroud the stack in bubble-wrap. Heat generated by the sprouting process itself will spur them on. Colder-climate seeds like peas, sunflower, brassica and wheat will sprout even at 50oF.

If you don't have electric power you could instead put a large water reservoir on top of the stack - and get up to a week's irrigation, automatically.

Plastic tanks from office water coolers are ideal. After the sixth use, the service firms have to shred them so they'll happily give you those old 22ltr empties free.

Fit a plastic hose below and clip it to deliver the exact volume of constant drip you need.

But uh, what do we do with all those sprouts?

Yeoman's First Rule of Healthy Eating is: "don't eat what you don't like".

Howsoever healthy, raw food is no gift to reprobates like me whose palate is vulcanised like an old car tyre. We can't enjoy it so we won't come back. So for starters here is:

Yeoman's Fresh Sprout-Green Muffins

This yields a fast-food breakfast or snack lunch and the fillings can be varied to your taste.

225g/8oz self-raising flour (wholewheat makes a denser, biscuit-type muffin)
1/4 tsp salt & a little pepper or kelp
1tbl vegetable oil
2 eggs
1-2 cups chopped sprout greens (include the pulses/seeds only if you want a chewy muffin)
180ml/6 fl oz milk or soy/seed milk

You could optionally add a cupful of grated chopped   bacon,   corned beef, cooked meat or poultry; lightly fried onions; cooked potato, pulses or rice.

Experiment with flavourings like mild herbs, soy or Worcester sauce. Or sprinkle grated cheese on top or (in the last few minutes) chopped olives or other pizza toppings.

Mix the dry ingredients. Add the sprouts (and any other fillings). Beat the eggs and milk briefly and mix in. Put into fairy-cake tins and bake at 200oC/400F/gas mark 6 or the top oven of an Aga for 20-25 minutes till brown.

For a fast breakfast, mix it the night before and bake while cleaning your teeth next morning. *Or* make an extra-wide muffin with a hole in the middle and drop in an egg during the last five minute's baking. **A healthy Egg McMuffin!** .

Fun variations on manually-watered sprouts:

* *A Sprout Tree.*

Take eight clean shallow tins, like tuna cans, their tops cut entirely off and bases perforated. Make a centre hole in the base of each. Thread together with plasticated string, and thread 3in sections of plastic drinking straw on the string between each can to keep them apart. Add pre-soaked seed.

Hang the Sprout Tree in your shower cabinet and spray it with the shower nozzle at dawn and dusk. (It works.)

*A Sprout Cake Tray.

Rescue an old-fashioned tiered cake stand from a charity shop. Spread kitchen paper circles on each plate. Cover with pre-soaked seed. Mist daily. **Result:** a table conversation piece that's your own little Hanging Garden of Babylon.

*A Sprout Pyramid.

A variation is to cut polystyrene ceiling tiles into progressively smaller squares. Make a pyramid. Adorn the flat surfaces with kitchen paper and proceed as above.

* Salad Side-Nibbles.

Plant seeds in individual ramikins, unlacquered bamboo baskets or other pretty serving dishes on a circle of kitchen paper, treble-thick - a different seed or pulse for each dish. Stagger your planting so eg. long-growing

sunflower greens are ready to cut on the same day as fast-cropping alfalfa.

Serve them at a dinner party by each plate, with a variety of dressings so guests can help themselves and mix and match.

Author, author....

John Yeoman - MA Hons (Oxon) under a different name - is the pseudonym of a total rogue. He started his career at the age of 23 peddling witchcraft cabarets in a cellar near Leicester Square (entrance 10 shillings), then descended to a job in public relations.

After setting up what became one of Britain's largest regional PR firms, and founding the PR courses at the C. Inst of Marketing, he looked for new depths to plumb - and retired in luxury to become a marketing trainer and consultant, working off his wife's kitchen table.

It was supposed to be a hobby but it quickly made him a multi-millionaire again (in Italian lira, at least). Because this meant *work*, and sometimes he had to wake up before midday, he retired from it at once - to a new career tending his compost heap.

He then published the best-selling *Self-Reliance*, from Hyden House (1999), having gifted the world already with a slurry of brilliant, but largely unread, business textbooks.

Now his organic beans are again bringing him millions - but of aphids. And he's happy. Because (unlike clients) aphids can be legally killed.

He lives with a super-genius wife and pre-teenage daughter (so bright, that they disdain Mensa membership), plus several hundred dim frogs in a 1/2 acre smallholding surrounded by Bottle Beds, tipis, Grow Poles and other organic detritus.

Forgive him while he slouches off now, to trounce his family at Scrabble. He points out "The strategic use of 'zucchini' can yield you... *150 points.*"

He humbly thanks you for reading this.

ALL YOU EVER WANTED TO KNOW ABOUT THE VILLAGE GUILD (BUT WERE, QUITE RIGHTLY, TOO LAZY TO ASK)

We're a little company that I run off an old Victorian washstand in my conservatory.

As I write this (in early Winter), I can see - on my right - cherry tomatoes, broad beans and nasturtiums growing lustily in my hydroponic beds. All are *totally* organic, fed exclusively with comfrey-nettle tea. Before me is a two-ton obelisk of plastic-clad books (this book), prettily shrouded in tinfoil. To reflect, of course, light on to the plants...

At my left, is 100 sq ft of little cabbages, lettuces, land cress and corn salad, enough for my family all Winter - growing *vertically* up my conservatory wall in plastic milk bottles.

Bubbling away in a corner, is my sprout machine - growing vitamin-rich sunflower and pea sprouts, all by itself.

We're a funny company.

When you call, fax or e-mail me , you actually get me (or, if I'm in the paddock, you might get Sarah, my answering machine). She has human feelings too. So do be nice.

The Village Guild is dedicated to showing you how to live a more self-reliant life. Get off the consumer treadmill. And - darn it - have *fun*. Contact us for subscription details of our extraordinary *Lazy Gardener* newsletter!

Further copies of this book are available at £11.90 (£13.90 outside the UK), incl p&p, from the publisher below. Visa & MasterCard accepted.

Phone/Fax: 01525 221492; **E-mail:** John@villageguild.co.uk
The Village Guild Ltd, The Old School House, Ivinghoe Aston, Leighton Buzzard, Beds, LU7 9DP, United Kingdom.

HOW TO ACQUIRE A *FREE* MANUAL!

'The Slug Secret'

To thank you for your courtesy in buying my little book (you *did* buy it, didn't you?), I have prepared a big FREE 32-page manual for you, **The Slug Secret**. This is 'the' definitive guide to 51 ingenious and tested ideas for ridding your garden of slugs and snails, *organically*.

It includes one idea so effective and outrageous, I *dare* you to try it!

To accept my manual by post - entirely free of charge, wherever you are in the world - merely write your mailing address below and return this page to me, post paid. *Or* a photocopy will suffice. *Or* merely write or e-mail me with your full snail-mail (*sorry!*) postal address, pleading "Please send me **The Slug Secret**".

No salesman (or mollusc) will call. You'll find my free manual very useful - *and enjoyable!*

Of course, if you have wisely acquired it already, you won't need yet *another*. Will you? (I find in my old age, one can acquire All Too Many Secrets...)

John Yeoman

Yes, John, please send me your *Slug Secret* manual, entirely free and without obligation

Surname   Initials   Dr/Rev/Mrs/Mr/Ms
Address

                                                              Postcode

Post to The Village Guild Ltd, The Old School House, Ivinghoe Aston, Leighton Buzzard, Beds LU7 9DP, UK.
Or e-mail: john@villageguild.co.uk